W9-BJH-880

7-8

SCHOLASTIC

Third Grade

Jumbo Workbook

This book belongs to

_____

No part of this publication may be reproduced in whole or in part, or stored in a retrieval system, or transmitted in any form or by any means, electronic, mechanical, photocopying, recording, or otherwise, without written permission of the publisher. For information regarding permission, write to Scholastic Inc., Attention: Permissions Dept., 557 Broadway, New York, NY 10012.

Cover design by Sequel Creative
Cover art by Patrick Girouard
Interior illustrations by Steve Cox, Micheal Denman, The Everett Collection, New York (page 98),
Kate Flanagan, Susan Hendron, Kathy Marlin, Mark Mason, Mike Moran, Neil Riley,
Peter Samek, Karen Sevaly, and Carol Tiernon

ISBN 978-0-545-91025-5

Copyright © 2005 Scholastic Inc.
All rights reserved. Printed in the U.S.A.

2 3 4 5 6 7 8 9 10 11 12 13 14   56   22 21 20 19 18

Dear Parents,

The power to succeed is in every child! The question is: How can you help your child achieve this success and become an independent, lifelong learner?

You have already taken the first step! This *Third Grade Jumbo Workbook* is the perfect way to support the learning your child needs to be successful in school.

Research shows that independent practice helps children gain mastery of essential skills. This book includes carefully selected, teacher-tested activities that give third graders exactly the practice they need. Topics covered include:

- Spelling and Grammar
- Vocabulary
- Reading Skills
- Writing
- Multiplication and Division
- Fractions and Decimals

You'll also find assessments to help you keep track of your child's progress—and provide important practice with standardized test formats.

Let's get started! Your involvement will make this a valuable educational experience and will support and enhance your child's learning.

Enjoy!

Hindie

Hindie Weissman
Educational Consultant,
27+ years teaching experience

GRADE 3 Learn and Succeed

Welcome!

Grade 3 is a critical stepping stone on the road to learning success! This workbook has been carefully designed to help ensure your child has the tools he or she needs to soar in school. On the 300-plus pages that follow, you'll find plenty of practice in each of these must-know curriculum areas:

SPELLING	READING SKILLS	VOCABULARY	GRAMMAR
• Recognizing Short & Long Vowel Spellings • Recognizing Unusual Vowel Sounds • Recognizing Commonly Misspelled Words • Spelling List	• Recognizing Main Idea/Details • Recognizing Cause/Effect • Using Context Clues • Identifying Story Elements	• Understanding Synonyms, Antonyms, Homonyms, Homophones & Homographs • Recognizing Compound Words • Learning Content Area Words • Understanding Analogies	• Recognizing Types of Sentences • Understanding Parts of Speech • Understanding Punctuation
WRITING	**ADDITION/SUBTRACTION**	**MULTIPLICATION/DIVISION**	**FRACTIONS/GRAPHS**
• Sentence Building • Combining and Expanding Sentences • Building Paragraphs	• Adding & Subtracting Multi-Digit Numbers	• Multiplying With Regrouping • Understanding Division • Solving Word Problems Using Multiplication & Division	• Identifying Fractions • Using Bar and Line Graphs • Ordering Pairs & Coordinates

Helping your child build essential skills is easy!

These teacher-approved activities have been specially developed to make learning both accessible and enjoyable. On each page, you'll find:

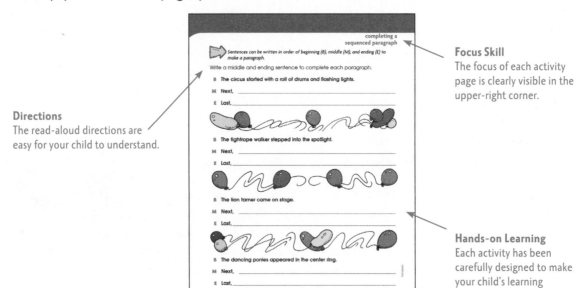

Directions
The read-aloud directions are easy for your child to understand.

Focus Skill
The focus of each activity page is clearly visible in the upper-right corner.

Hands-on Learning
Each activity has been carefully designed to make your child's learning meaningful, hands-on, and fun.

Scholastic

with Scholastic!

These great extras are guaranteed to make learning extra engaging!

This workbook is loaded with lots of motivating, special components including:

SPECIAL ACTIVITIES TO GET READY FOR FOURTH GRADE ▶

Give your child a head start in fourth grade with this BONUS assortment of get-ready activities.

◀ ### CONNECTION TO ONLINE LEARNING

Boost computer literacy with this special link to a treasury of skill-building online activities at www.scholastic.com/success.

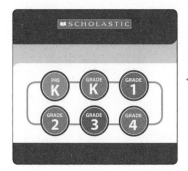

MOTIVATING STICKERS ▶

Mark the milestones of your child's learning path with these bright, kid-pleasing stickers.

◀ ### INSTANT FLASH CARDS

Promote reading fluency with these fun flash cards.

REWARD CERTIFICATE ▶

Celebrate your child's leap in learning with this colorful, pull-out completion certificate.

◀ ### LIST OF THE BEST BOOKS FOR YOUNG LEARNERS

Reinforce key concepts and build a love of reading with this great list of learning-rich books selected by top educators. See page 12.

QUICK ASSESSMENT TESTS ▶

Make sure your child *really* masters each must-know skill with the instant assessment tests that conclude each section.

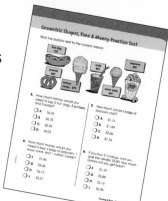

Scholastic

Table of Contents

Scholastic

Scholastic

MATHEMATICS

Scholastic

Tips for Success

Here are some tips to help your child get the most out of this workbook:

- Provide a quiet, comfortable place for your child to work.

- Make sure your child understands the directions.

- Encourage your child to use colorful pencils and markers to make learning fun.

- Check completed work as soon as possible and review corrected work with your child.

- Pay attention to areas where your child is having difficulty. Spend extra time to help him or her master those skills.

- Provide a special area at home where your child's work can be displayed.

- Be positive and encouraging. Praise your child for his or her efforts and good work.

Scholastic

Read with Your Child

Reading to your child and having him or her read to you is an extremely effective way of supporting your child's learning. When you read with him or her, make sure your child is actively participating. Here are five ways to support your child's reading:

1. Let your child choose the book.

2. Look at the cover of the book and ask your child what he or she thinks the story will be about.

3. As you read the book, locate a good stopping point and ask your child to predict what will happen next. Then read to confirm the prediction or correct it.

4. Discuss the characters in the story: Are they kind? good? bad? clever? Are they like characters in another book?

5. When you finish the story, have your child retell it.

Scholastic

Read with Your Child

Looking for a great book to read with your child? Here are some top teacher picks:

- *Bunnicula* by Deborah and James Howe (Aladdin, 1996).

- *Dear Mr. Henshaw* by Beverly Cleary (HarperCollins, 1983).

- *Favorite Greek Myths* by Mary Pope Osborne (Scholastic Press, 1989).

- *First in the Field: Baseball Hero Jackie Robinson* by Derek T. Dingle (Hyperion, 1998).

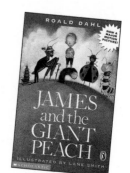

- *James and the Giant Peach* by Roald Dahl (Alfred A. Knopf, 1961).

- *Justin and the Best Biscuits in the World* by Mildred Pitts Walter (HarperCollins, 1986).

- *My Name Is Georgia: A Portrait* by Jeannette Winter (Silver Whistle, 1998).

- *The Music of Dolphins* by Karen Hesse (Scholastic, 1996).

- *Stone Fox* by John Reynolds Gardiner (HarperTrophy, 1980).

- *Wayside School Is Falling Down* by Louis Sachar (HarperTrophy, 1998).

Scholastic

The Alphabet in Cursive

Learning to write in cursive brings your child the delightful sense, "I'm growing up!" In this section, children transfer their knowledge of letters and the sounds they make from manuscript handwriting to the cursive alphabet.

What to Do
Have your child use pen, pencil, or markers on the letter-writing practice pages to trace and write the letters. Then have your child write the words and the sentence in cursive. When finished, invite him or her to circle their "best" upper- and lowercase letters.

Keep On Going!
Encourage your child to use cursive handwriting to write invitations, thank-you notes, or friendly letters to friends and family members.

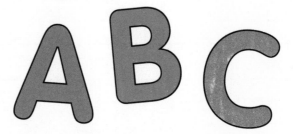

Aa

Trace and write.

a a

a a

Aa

Atlantic

ape   apple

Active ants awaken

angry Asian aardvarks.

Scholastic

Bb

Trace and write.

B   B

b   b

Bb

Baltimore

baby   boy

Beautiful baboons blow

bubbles   in   a   bathtub.

Cc

Trace and write.

C C

c c

Cc

Cincinnati

candy   case

Confident camels carry

cute, cuddly cats.

Scholastic

Dd

Trace and write.

D D

d d

Dd

Detroit

dandy   dirt

Daring dogs decide

to drive to Dallas.

Scholastic

Ee

Trace and write.

E E

e e

Ee

Erie

ever   eye

Elderly, elegant elephants

eagerly eat eggs.

Scholastic

Ff

Trace and write.

F F

f f

F f

Fenton

five   fast

Frisky foxes frequently

fumble footballs.

Scholastic

$\mathscr{G}g$

Trace and write.

$\mathscr{G}$ $\mathscr{G}$

g g

$\mathscr{G}g$

Green Bay

gauge   grate

Giggling geese gobble

giant green gumballs.

Scholastic

Hh

Trace and write.

H H H

h h

Hh

Hanover

honor   halt

Happy hamsters have

huge, hilarious hats.

Ii

Trace and write.

I I

i i

Ii

Inglewood

ink   ill

Idle inchworms ignore

irate insects in Iowa.

Scholastic

J j

Trace and write.

J   J

j   j

J j

Joliet

jump   jet

Jaguars juggle jars of

jelly beans in January.

K k

Trace and write.

K K

k k

K k

Kenosha

kite   kick

Kind kangaroos knit

knickers for kids.

Scholastic

Ll

Trace and write.

L L

l l

Ll

Littleton

lock   little

Large, lazy lobsters

lounge leisurely.

Scholastic

M m

Trace and write.

M M

m m

M m

Missoula

miss   movie

Many merry mice

make mushy meatballs.

Scholastic

Nn

Trace and write.

n n

n n

N n

Newton

navy   next

Nine nocturnal newts

navigate north nightly.

Scholastic

Oo

Trace and write.

O O

o o

Oo

Omaha

over   oblong

Odorous otters order

olive oil over oysters.

Scholastic

Pp

Trace and write.

P P

p p

Pp

Princeton

pipe   parrot

Pretty pigs pop popcorn

perfectly in Pittsburgh.

Scholastic

Q q

Trace and write.

Q Q

q q

Q q

Quincy

quick   quit

Quaint queens quilt

quickly and quietly.

Scholastic

Rr

Trace and write.

R R

r r

Rr

Rochester

rich   rear

Restless reindeer run

races rapidly in Reno.

Scholastic

Ss

Trace and write.

S S S

s s

Ss

Seattle

sense   safe

Sleepy spiders sell

smelly skunk soap.

Scholastic

Tt

Trace and write.

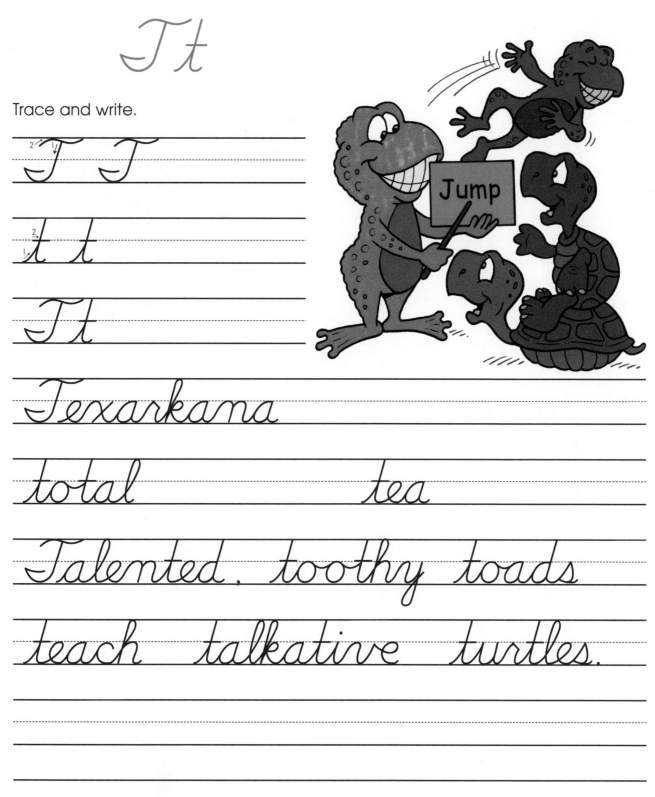

T T

t t

Tt

Texarkana

total   tea

Talented, toothy toads

teach talkative turtles.

Scholastic

U u

Trace and write.

U U

u u

U u

Urbana

utter   *use*

Uniformed umpires

usher upset unicorns.

Scholastic

$\mathcal{V}v$

Trace and write.

$\mathcal{V}$ $\mathcal{V}$

v v

$\mathcal{V}v$

$\mathcal{V}ancouver$

$vivid$ $vase$

$\mathcal{V}ain$ $vultures$

$vacuum$ $vigorously.$

Scholastic

Ww

Trace and write.

W W

w w

Ww

Westover

women   wow

Wiggly worms wander

westward with whistles.

Scholastic

Xx

Trace and write.

X X

x x

Xx

Xenia

axis   exit

Xavier Ox x-rayed

six extra xylophones.

Y y

Trace and write.

Y Y

y y

Yy

Yorktown

yacht   yet

Youthful yaks yell.

"Yeah, yellow yo-yos!"

Scholastic

Z z

Trace and write.

Z Z

Z Z

Z Z

Zanesville

zipper   *zero*

Zany zebras zigzag

zestfully to Zimbabwe.

ZIMBABWE

Scholastic

A–Z

A B C D E F G
H I J K L M
N O P Q R S T
U V W X Y Z

Write.

_____
- - - - - - - - - - - - - - - - -
_____

_____
- - - - - - - - - - - - - - - - -
_____

_____
- - - - - - - - - - - - - - - - -
_____

_____
- - - - - - - - - - - - - - - - -
_____

Scholastic

Our Solar System

The sun is the center of our solar system. It is the only star in our solar system. The planets and their moons all orbit the sun. The sun provides heat and light to the planets and their moons.

Write.

_____

- - - - - - - - - - - - - - - - - - -

_____

- - - - - - - - - - - - - - - - - - -

_____

- - - - - - - - - - - - - - - - - - -

_____

- - - - - - - - - - - - - - - - - - -

_____

- - - - - - - - - - - - - - - - - - -

_____

- - - - - - - - - - - - - - - - - - -

_____

- - - - - - - - - - - - - - - - - - -

_____

Scholastic

Ancient Astronomers

People who study the sun, moon, planets, and stars are called astronomers. Cave people were some of the first astronomers. They drew the different shapes of the moon on the walls of their caves. Long ago, sailors studied the stars to help them travel. The ancient Greeks studied many of the planets.

Write.

Scholastic

What Is a Year?

A year is the time it takes for a planet to orbit the sun. A year on Earth is 365 days. It only takes Mercury 88 days to make a trip around the sun. However, it takes Uranus 84 Earth years and Neptune 165 Earth years to orbit the sun one time.

Write.

_____

_____

_____

_____

_____

_____

_____

_____

_____

_____

_____

Scholastic

Beautiful Venus

Venus is the easiest planet to see in the sky because it is the closest to Earth. It is sometimes called the Evening Star. The Romans named Venus after their goddess of love and beauty. Venus is so hot, it could melt lead. It has an orange sky.

Write.

_____

_____

_____

_____

_____

_____

_____

_____

_____

_____

_____

_____

_____

_____

Scholastic

King Jupiter

Jupiter is the largest planet. It is so big that 1,300 Earths could fit inside of it! That is why the Romans named it after the king of the Roman gods. Jupiter spins faster than all the other planets.

Write.

Scholastic

Cursive Alphabet Practice Test

Fill in the bubble next to the correct answer.

Example

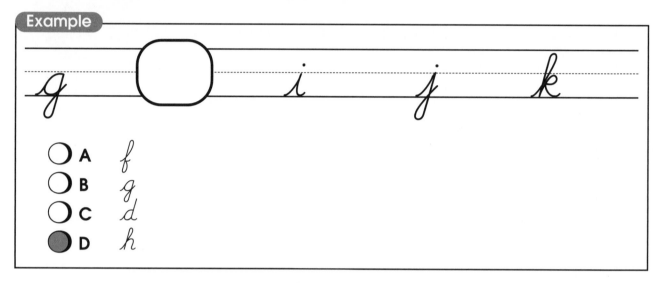

- ○ **A** f
- ○ **B** g
- ○ **C** d
- ● **D** h

1. Fill in the bubble next to the missing letter.

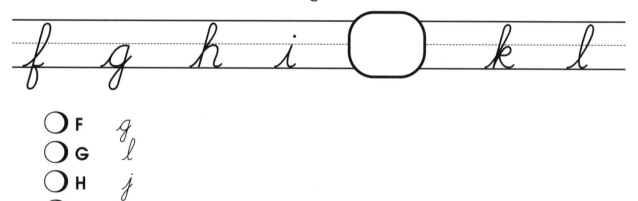

- ○ **F** g
- ○ **G** l
- ○ **H** j
- ○ **J** m

2. Fill in the bubble next to the missing letters.

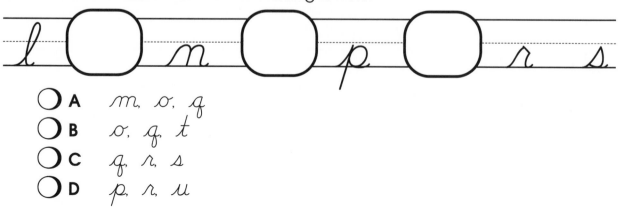

- ○ **A** m, o, q
- ○ **B** o, q, t
- ○ **C** q, r, s
- ○ **D** p, r, u

Scholastic

Cursive Alphabet Practice Test

Fill in the bubble next to the correct answer.

3. Which word would you find first in a dictionary?

⭕ **A** apple

⭕ **B** around

⭕ **C** away

⭕ **D** add

4. Which word would you find first in a dictionary?

⭕ **F** next

⭕ **G** right

⭕ **H** easy

⭕ **J** fit

5. Which word would come last in a dictionary?

⭕ **A** cap

⭕ **B** cape

⭕ **C** capable

⭕ **D** cable

Scholastic

Spelling

In this section your child reviews the spelling of long and short vowels and the unusual spelling of beginning letter sounds. He or she will also be introduced to commonly misspelled words. The section starts with palindromes. Those are words that are spelled the same way backward and forward.

What to Do

Have your child complete the activity pages. Review your child's answers. Remember, answers to the activities are in the back of the book if you need them.

The last page in this section is the Grade 3 spelling list. Review these words with your child throughout the year.

Keep On Going!

Play a spelling game with your child. Say:
I am thinking of a word.

> It begins with the hard-*g* sound
> It has a long-*a* vowel.
> It ends with a *t* sound.
> It has a silent *e* at the end.
> Say the word and spell it. [gate]

Take turns giving and receiving clues.

gate

Read this question: Was it a cat I saw? Now read it backward. Notice that it reads the same way. The title is a palindrome. **Palindromes** *are words, phrases, or sentences that can be read forward or backward.*

noon	bib	kayak
eve	mum	race car
pop	dud	solos
pup	gag	toot

Write the missing palindrome from the box above in each sentence. Then reread each sentence. Can you find the other palindrome in each one? Underline the word.

1. It is a good thing you put a _____ on the tot because she just spilled her soup.

2. What did you think of the two _____ I sang at the concert?

3. Hannah taught her _____ to sit up and roll over.

4. My dad has to work until _____ this Saturday.

5. The soup Bob made was so bad that it almost made me _____.

6. "Would you care for coffee, tea, or _____, Madam?" the waiter asked.

7. Otto heard the train whistle _____ four times.

8. "You speed like a _____ driver!" Ava complained.

9. Refer to page 6 of your manual to learn how to paddle a _____.

10. Anna got the last ferry from the island on the _____ of the terrible storm.

11. "Keep _____ and do not say a word," ordered Mom.

12. Nan thought the movie was a _____.

Scholastic

The **short-**a **sound** *is often spelled with the letter* a.
The **long-***a* **sound** *can be spelled with the letters* a_e, ai, *or* ay.

A. Read and write each word. Then organize the list words by the spelling of
their *a* sound.

 List Words

1. dragon _____   short *a*   *ai*

2. today _____ _____ _____

3. brave _____ _____ _____

4. plains _____ _____ _____

5. mistake _____

6. raise _____   *a_e*   *ay*

7. maybe _____ _____ _____

8. dance _____ _____ _____

9. wait _____ _____ _____

10. holiday _____

11. handle _____

12. became _____

Challenge Words

13. parade _____

14. costume _____

15. balloons _____

B. Write four list words that have three vowels (not including y).

_____ _____ _____ _____

Scholastic

A. Proofread the letter. Circle the six misspelled words. Write them correctly on the lines below.

Dear Chelsey,

Chinese New Year is almost here! It is celebrated in January or February. The date of the holliday depends on the movement of the moon. The children in my family wate all year to receive red paper envelopes full of money from our family and friends. My favorite part of the celebration is the parade. This year my braive brother will wear the dragin costume with some of his friends. They will danse through the streets to entertain the crowds. Maybee one day you can visit during this wonderful celebration.

Your friend,
Mia

_____ _____ _____

_____ _____ _____

B. Write the list word for each definition. The shaded boxes will answer the riddle.

Where do dragons go to dance?

1. an error
2. to lift
3. to move to music
4. the past tense of *become*
5. the present time
6. open rolling land
7. part that can be grabbed to help move something

C. Find and circle the challenge words. Write them on the lines.

_____

_____

_____

Scholastic

Reading & Math • Grade 3

The **short**-e **sound** *is often spelled with the letter* e.
The **long**-e **sound** *can be spelled with the letters* ea *or* ee.

Read and write each word. Then organize the list words
by the spelling of their *e* sound.

A. List Words

1. scream _____   short *e*   *ea*

2. cheek _____ _____ _____

3. member _____ _____ _____

4. freeze _____ _____ _____

5. next _____ _____ _____

6. reason _____

7. asleep _____   *ee*

8. check _____ _____

9. team _____ _____

10. enter _____ _____

11. between _____ _____

12. reach _____

Challenge Words

13. basketball _____

14. soccer _____

15. tennis _____

B. Write four list words that begin with more than one consonant.

_____ _____ _____ _____

Scholastic

A. Use a list word to complete each analogy.

1. *Push* is to *pull* as *exit* is to _____.

2. *Sing* is to *joyful* as _____ is to *scared*.

3. *Puddle* is to *melt* as *ice* is to _____.

4. *Teacher* is to *class* as *coach* is to _____.

5. *Sister* is to *family* as _____ is to *group*.

6. *Narrow* is to *wide* as _____ is to *awake*.

B. Circle each of the list words hidden in the puzzle. The words go across, down, backward, and diagonally. Write each word in the correct group.

r	k	c	e	h	c	n	o	d	g	m
b	a	r	i	s	c	r	e	a	m	e
e	r	r	f	g	r	a	b	x	y	n
t	a	e	s	r	m	a	e	t	t	t
w	h	a	a	s	e	a	n	d	a	e
e	d	c	i	s	m	e	m	b	e	r
e	s	h	x	c	o	t	z	t	l	i
n	c	h	e	e	k	n	l	e	g	r
a	v	m	a	p	e	e	l	s	a	c

Across _____ _____ _____

Backward _____ _____

Down _____ _____ _____

Diagonally _____ _____

C. Find a word in each sentence that could be replaced by a challenge word. Cross it out and write the challenge word on the line.

7. Mike kicked the big ball down the field and into the net. _____

8. Kayla won the chess match last Friday. _____

9. Sam grabbed the ball and shot it through the hoop. _____

The **short-**i **sound** *is often spelled with the letter* i.
The **long-**i **sound** *can be spelled with the letters* i_e *or* igh.

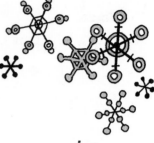

A. Read and write each word. Then organize the list
words by the spelling of their *i* sound.

 **List Words**

		short *i*	i_e
1.	winter	_____	_____
2.	surprise	_____	_____
3.	bright	_____	_____
4.	middle	_____	_____
5.	polite	_____	_____
6.	frighten	_____	
7.	children	_____	*igh*
8.	tight	_____	_____
9.	while	_____	_____
10.	strike	_____	_____
11.	kitchen	_____	_____
12.	slight	_____	

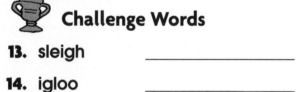 **Challenge Words**

13. sleigh _____

14. igloo _____

15. icicle _____

B. Write four list words that end in silent *e*.

_____ _____ _____ _____

Scholastic

A.  Write the list word that belongs with each group.

1. kind, considerate, _____

2. ball, foul, _____

3. scare, startle, _____

4. family room, bathroom, _____

5. mother, father, _____

6. autumn, summer, _____

B.  Look at the shape of the list words. Write the
word that fits in each set of letter boxes.

7.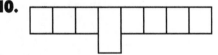

8.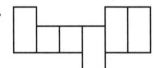

9.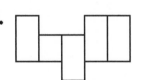

10.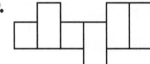

11.

12.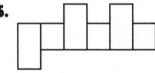

13.

14.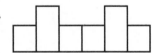

15.

C. Write the challenge word that matches each picture.

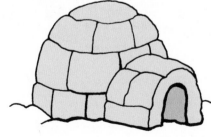

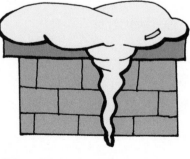

16. _____

17. _____

18. _____

Scholastic

The **short-o sound** *is often spelled with the letter* o.
The **long-o sound** *can be spelled with the
letters* o_e *or* ow.

A. Read and write each word. Then organize the list
words by the spelling of their *o* sound.

 List Words   short *o*   o_e

1. pillow _____   _____   _____

2. rocket _____   _____   _____

3. alone _____   _____   _____

4. below _____   _____   _____

5. monster _____

6. globe _____   *ow*

7. follow _____   _____

8. holler _____   _____

9. whole _____   _____

10. window _____

11. bottle _____   short *o* and *ow*

12. suppose _____   _____

Challenge Words

13. feathers _____

14. blanket _____

15. trouble _____

B. Write four list words that have double consonants.

_____   _____   _____   _____

Scholastic

A. Use list words to complete the story.

Pillow fights are the greatest! The best pillow fight I ever had was with my

brother. He threw his _____ so hard that it flew over my head like

a _____ into space. Seconds later, I heard my mom

_____, "Stop throwing the pillows. One may fly out the

_____!" I couldn't resist. I blasted my pillow toward my brother. I

missed my aim, and it broke a _____ _____ of my

mom's perfume. I don't _____ we'll have any more pillow fights

around here!

B. Complete the crossword puzzle using the list word that fits each clue.

Across
3. complete
8. rhymes with *hollow*
9. spaceship
10. a noun you can look through
11. antonym for *together*
12. a scary creature

Down
1. the world
2. antonym for *above*
4. to shout
5. a soft place for your head
6. a glass container
7. rhymes with *grows*

C. Write the challenge words in alphabetical order.

1. _____ 2. _____ 3. _____

 The **short-**u **sound** *is often spelled with the letter* u.
The /o͞o/ **sound** *can be spelled with the letters* u, oo, *or* ou.

A. Read and write each word. Then organize the list
words by the spelling of their *u* sound.

 List Words

		short *u*	long *u*
1. super	_____		
2. coupon	_____	_____	_____
3. until	_____	_____	_____
4. loose	_____	_____	_____
5. ruler	_____		
6. group	_____	o͞o	ou
7. shampoo	_____	_____	_____
8. number	_____	_____	_____
9. soup	_____	_____	_____
10. sudden	_____		
11. duty	_____		
12. caboose	_____		

 Challenge Words

13. groceries _____

14. shopping _____

15. supermarket _____

B. A noun is a word that names a person,
place, or thing. Write four list words that are nouns.

_____ _____ _____ _____

Scholastic

A. Write the list word that completes each sentence in the puzzle. Then write the letters in the shaded boxes in order to spell the name of a grocery item.

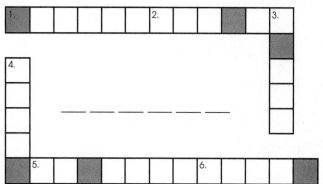

1. Mom used a _____ to save a dollar on the price of a ticket.

2. Molly's _____ showed that her plant had grown three inches.

3. A _____ of fish is called a school.

4. Spot's collar was too _____, and he squirmed out of it.

5. Always _____ your hair after swimming.

6. The beach party was great fun _____ it started raining.

B. Write two list words that share a common letter to complete each puzzle.

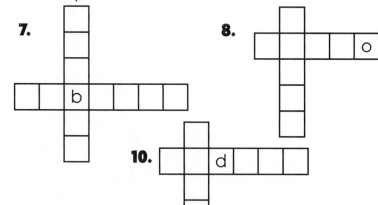

7.   8.   9.

10.   11.

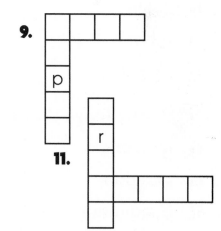

C. Guide words are listed at the top of each page in a dictionary. They show the first and last words found on that page. Write each challenge word on the dictionary page where it would be found.

| sunset • supply | grizzly • grouch | shoe • shortage |

Scholastic

The /ô/ **sound** *as in* paw *can be spelled* au, aw, *or* augh.

A. Read and write each word. Then organize the list words by their *ô* sound spelling.

 List Words

au   *aw*

1. hawk _____

2. daughter _____   _____   _____

3. awful _____   _____   _____

4. because _____   _____   _____

5. naughty _____   _____   _____

6. pause _____

7. caught _____   *augh*

8. dawn _____   _____

9. sauce _____   _____

10. author _____   _____

11. crawl _____   _____

12. taught _____

Challenge Words

13. food chain _____

14. producer _____

15. consumer _____

B. Write four list words that will be tough to learn to spell.

_____   _____   _____   _____

Scholastic

A. Use list words to complete the paragraph.

The Hawk's Prey

I read an article about red-tailed hawks today. The _____ was a scientist who had studied a hawk that he named Harry. Harry is a bird of prey. _____ he has sharp talons and incredible speed, he can easily catch other small animals. The article showed a picture of Harry as he _____ a mouse in the field at _____. Red-tailed hawks like Harry can fly for hundreds of miles without getting tired. They _____ from flapping their wings and glide in the wind. If you are interested in learning more about _____s, check out the book *Birds of Prey*. It _____ me a lot about hawks.

B. Use the code to spell a list word.

1	2	3	4	5	6	7	8	9	10	11	12	13	14	15
a	c	d	e	f	g	h	l	n	r	s	t	u	w	y

1. _____
2 - 1 - 13 - 6 - 7 - 12

2. _____
2 - 10 - 1 - 14 - 8

3. _____
9 - 1 - 13 - 6 - 7 - 12 - 15

4. _____
3 - 1 - 13 - 6 - 7 - 12 - 4 - 10

5. _____
12 - 1 - 13 - 6 - 7 - 12

6. _____
11 - 1 - 13 - 2 - 4

7. _____
1 - 14 - 5 - 13 - 8

C. Use the letters in each challenge word to spell two smaller words. For example, the letters in *daughter* could be used to spell *the* and *hat*.

food chain	producer	consumer
_____	_____	_____
_____	_____	_____

Scholastic

The /s/ **sound** is sometimes spelled with the letter c.
The /j/ **sound** is sometimes spelled with the letter g.

A. Read and write each word. Then organize the list words by their sounds.

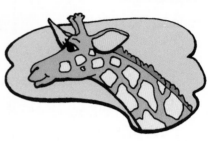

 List Words

		"c" spellings that sound like /s/	"g" spellings that sound like /j/
1. giant	_____		
2. giraffe	_____		
3. office	_____	_____	_____
4. excite	_____	_____	_____
5. strange	_____	_____	_____
6. fence	_____	_____	_____
7. gentle	_____	_____	_____
8. center	_____	_____	_____
9. since	_____		
10. danger	_____		
11. large	_____		
12. price	_____		

🏆 **Challenge Words**

13. monkey _____

14. antelope _____

15. elephant _____

B. 👓 An adjective is a describing word. Write four list words that could be used to describe an animal.

_____   _____   _____   _____

Scholastic

A. Proofread the report. Circle the eight misspelled words. Then write them correctly on the lines below.

Our Class Trip

What a great field trip! We went to the city zoo to observe grassland animals. The most interesting was the geraff. I didn't expect such a larg animal to be so jentle. I picked a dandelion and held it over the fense toward the giraffe. It strolled over and stretched its neck to smell the senter of the flower. It must have known that there was no danjer because it wrapped its gient tongue around the dandelion and took it right out of my hand! It was such a stranje feeling! I can't wait to go back!

_____   _____   _____

_____   _____   _____

_____   _____

B. Write the list word for each definition. The shaded boxes will answer the riddle.

What do you call a giraffe's necklace?

1. big; rhymes with barge

2. a place where business occurs

3. in a kind manner

4. odd

5. something that may cause harm

6. to stir up

7. from then until now

8. cost

C. Find and circle the challenge words hidden in the maze. Write them on the lines.

_____

_____

_____

Scholastic

When a word ends with one vowel and one consonant (VC), double the consonant before adding an ending. *For example,* run *becomes* running. *When a word ends with a silent* e, *the* e *is dropped before adding an ending. For example,* rake *becomes* raking.

A. Read and write each word. Then organize the list words by their endings.

List Words

		-er ending	**-est ending**
1. swimmer	_____		
2. wisest	_____	_____	_____
3. hoped	_____	_____	_____
4. shopping	_____	_____	_____
5. clapped	_____		
6. safer	_____	**-ed ending**	**-ing ending**
7. biggest	_____	_____	_____
8. getting	_____	_____	_____
9. freezer	_____	_____	_____
10. coming	_____		
11. stopped	_____		
12. whitest	_____		

Challenge Words

13. champion _____

14. medal _____

15. compete _____

B. Write four list words that have long vowel sounds.

_____   _____   _____   _____

Scholastic

A. Read each base word and write its matching list word with an ending. Then check the rule that applies to each word.

Base Word	List Word	Double the final consonant.	Drop the silent e.
1. big			
2. hope			
3. come			
4. get			
5. white			
6. wise			

B. Write a list word to complete each sentence. The shaded boxes will answer the riddle.

What did the sneezing champion win at the Olympics?

1. Are you _____ over today?

2. We are _____ for new shoes.

3. We _____ at the end of the show.

4. Our bus _____ at the corner.

5. My best friend is a strong _____.

6. Let's get ice cream from the _____.

7. I _____ my mother would agree.

8. Riding a bike is _____ with a helmet.

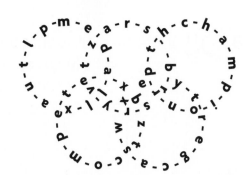
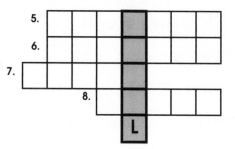

C. Find and circle the challenge words hidden in the Olympic rings. Write them on the lines.

_____

_____

_____

Scholastic

Some words do not follow common spelling patterns. Their spellings must be memorized.

A. Read and write each word. Then write an idea that will help you memorize each spelling. For example, *been* has two *e*'s.

 List Words

1. been   _____   _____

2. other   _____   _____

3. favorite   _____   _____

4. does   _____   _____

5. these   _____   _____

6. before   _____   _____

7. friend   _____   _____

8. always   _____   _____

9. their   _____   _____

10. done   _____   _____

11. people   _____   _____

12. thought   _____

Challenge Words

13. mammal   _____

14. canines   _____

15. breed   _____

B. Write four list words that will be the toughest to learn to spell.

_____   _____   _____   _____

Scholastic

A. Write the list word that belongs in each group.

1. this, those, _____

2. finished, completed, _____

3. especially liked, preferred, _____

4. pal, comrade, _____

5. _____, during, after

6. _____, sometimes, never

7. his, her, our, _____

8. persons, humans, _____

B. Write a list word that fits in the letter boxes. Use a list word only once.

9.

10.

11.

12.

13.

14.

15.

16.

17.

18.

C. Find the word in the sentence that could be replaced by a challenge word. Cross it out and write the challenge word on the line.

19. The elephant is the largest living animal. _____

20. Labrador retrievers are an excellent kind of dog for families.

_____

21. Dogs are used to help guard, herd, track, and hunt. _____

Scholastic

The /ôr/ **sound** *can be spelled with the letters* our.
The /ûr/ **sound** *can be spelled with the letters* ear *or* ur.

A. Read and write each word. Then organize the list words by their spellings.

List Words

1. search   _____   **/ôr/ spelled** *our*   **/ûr/ spelled** *ear*

2. pearl   _____   _____   _____

3. court   _____   _____   _____

4. purse   _____   _____   _____

5. pour   _____   _____   _____

6. Earth   _____

7. turtle   _____   **/ûr/ spelled** *ur*

8. fourth   _____   _____

9. early   _____   _____

10. burn   _____   _____

11. course   _____   _____

12. hurry   _____

Challenge Words

13. seashell   _____

14. oyster   _____

15. octopus   _____

B. Write four list words that can be verbs.

_____   _____   _____   _____

Scholastic

A. Write the list word that belongs in each group.

1. look, seek, _____

2. drizzle, rain, _____

3. snake, lizard, _____

4. late, on time, _____

5. Mars, Venus, _____

6. ruby, diamond, _____

7. handbag, pouch, _____

8. path, track, _____

B. Write a list word that fits in the letter boxes.

9.

10.

11.

12.

13.

14.

15.

16.

17.

C. Write the challenge word that matches each picture.

18. _____

19. _____

20. _____

Scholastic

The /âr/ **sound** *can be spelled with the letters* air, are, *or* ear.

A. Read and write each word. Then organize the list words by their spellings.

List Words

		/âr/ spelled air	**/âr/ spelled are**
1. rare	_____		
2. pear	_____	_____	_____
3. fair	_____	_____	_____
4. share	_____	_____	_____
5. stairs	_____	_____	_____
6. tear	_____		

/âr/ spelled ear

7. repair	_____	_____
8. scare	_____	_____
9. bear	_____	_____
10. careful	_____	_____
11. chair	_____	_____
12. wear	_____	

Challenge Words

13. orange _____

14. pineapple _____

15. watermelon _____

B. Write three list words that rhyme but have different spellings for the /âr/ sound.

_____ _____ _____

Scholastic

A. Use list words to complete the newspaper article.

It's Unbelievable!

A small girl has saved a _____ tree in Evergreen Park! The tree

was supposed to be cut down to build new apartments, but Lilly Butler

wouldn't allow it. "This _____ tree is special because of the fruit it

grows. The pears are sweet and juicy. It wouldn't be _____ to cut

it down," Lilly said. When she heard of plans to destroy the tree, Lilly climbed

to the top like a _____. She was _____ not to fall as she

found a safe branch to sit on like a _____. Lilly made her point. The

builders agreed not to _____ down the tree after all.

B. Complete the crossword puzzle using the list word that fits each clue.

Across
1. cautious
5. synonym for *steps*
7. a place to sit
8. to put on
9. a mammal

Down
2. to fix something that is broken
3. honest
4. homophone for *pair*
5. to split with a friend
6. to frighten
10. unusual

C. Use a dictionary to help you divide each of the challenge words into syllables. For example, the word *fairy* has two syllables: *fair-y*

1. _____   2. _____   3. _____

Scholastic

Throughout the year, see if you can learn all the words on this Grade 3 spelling list.

afternoon	chair	empty	homework	pair	skateboard	thought
alone	chasing	enough	hoped	pause	skipping	tight
along	check	enter	hurries	pear	slight	today
alphabet	cheek	everything	hurry	pearl	some	tries
always	children	excite	in	people	someone	turtle
ankle	clapped	fair	kitchen	pillow	something	twinkle
aren't	close	favorite	km	plains	soup	until
asleep	clothes	fence	knew	pocket	springtime	upstairs
author	cm	finish	knife	police	stairs	wait
aware	coming	flour	knock	polite	state	wasn't
awful	cough	flower	knot	pour	stopped	way
bear	couldn't	follow	known	price	strange	wear
beautiful	coupon	fourth	large	purse	straw	weigh
became	course	freeze	laugh	raise	strike	we've
because	court	freezer	laundry	rare	string	where's
been	crawl	fried	lazily	reach	strong	while
before	craziest	friend	loose	reason	sudden	whitest
belong	cries	frighten	married	repair	sum	whole
below	curve	funnier	match	replied	summer	window
beneath	dance	gentle	maybe	rocket	super	winter
between	danger	getting	member	ruler	suppose	wisest
biggest	daughter	giant	middle	safer	sure	wood
birthday	dawn	giraffe	midnight	sauce	surprise	worried
blink	delay	globe	mistake	scare	swimmer	would
bluebird	divide	graph	monster	scariest	swing	wouldn't
bottle	does	group	naughty	scream	taught	wren
brave	doesn't	handle	new	search	team	wrist
breakfast	done	happily	next	shadow	tear	write
bright	dragon	haven't	notebook	shampoo	telephone	wrong
bring	drank	hawk	nothing	share	thank	you'll
burn	drink	hear	number	she's	that's	youth
caboose	duty	heard	office	shopping	their	you've
careful	earlier	here	other	shouldn't	these	
caught	early	holiday	outdoors	sidewalk	they'll	
center	Earth	holler	page	since	think	

Scholastic

Spelling Practice Test

Fill in the bubble next to the correct answer.

1. Which word is a palindrome?

  ○ **A**   Sam

  ○ **B**   Anna

  ○ **C**   Ivy

  ○ **D**   Tom

2. Which word does NOT have a long-*a* sound?

  ○ **F**   make

  ○ **G**   boat

  ○ **H**   bay

  ○ **J**   wait

3. Which word has the short-*a* sound?

  ○ **A**   bait

  ○ **B**   brave

  ○ **C**   handle

  ○ **D**   gray

Scholastic

Spelling Practice Test

Fill in the bubble next to the correct answer.

4. Which word does NOT have the long-*e* sound?

  ⭘ **A**   between

  ⭘ **B**   reason

  ⭘ **C**   reach

  ⭘ **D**   check

5. Which word does NOT have the long-*o* sound?

  ⭘ **F**   whole

  ⭘ **G**   suppose

  ⭘ **H**   window

  ⭘ **J**   bottle

6. Which word has a long-*i* sound?

  ⭘ **A**   trouble

  ⭘ **B**   middle

  ⭘ **C**   while

  ⭘ **D**   kitchen

Scholastic

Spelling Practice Test

Fill in the bubble next to the correct answer.

7. Which word has the long-*u* sound?

   ○ **A**   fur

   ○ **B**   sudden

   ○ **C**   youth

   ○ **D**   full

8. Which word is NOT a compound word?

   ○ **F**   butterfly

   ○ **G**   present

   ○ **H**   birthday

   ○ **J**   sunset

9. Which word is a contraction for will not?

   ○ **A**   won't

   ○ **B**   willn't

   ○ **C**   wiln't

   ○ **D**   none of the above

Scholastic

Spelling Practice Test

Fill in the bubble next to the correct answer.

10. Which word has the /j/ sound as in the word *giraffe*?

○ **A**   gate

○ **B**   glamour

○ **C**   grid

○ **D**   gentle

11. Which word is spelled correctly?

○ **F**   mammel

○ **G**   uther

○ **H**   breded

○ **J**   canines

12. Which word is spelled correctly?

○ **A**   befor

○ **B**   peeple

○ **C**   allways

○ **D**   favorite

Scholastic

Reading Skills &
Reading Comprehension

Your child can become a strong reader by using key reading skills to make meaning out of what he or she reads. Good readers set a purpose when reading: to find the main idea, to discover important details, to find the sequence of the story, to compare and contrast story events or characters, to make inferences, predictions, or to draw conclusions. These key reading skills will help improve your child's comprehension of both fiction and non-fiction selections.

What to Do
Read the directions on each activity page with your child and have your child complete the activity. Then together check the work. Answers, when needed, are provided at the back of the workbook.

After your child reads the reading comprehension selections, have him or her answer the questions to test his or her comprehension.

Keep On Going!
Read a book or watch a TV show with your child. At good stopping points ask questions such as: *What do you think will happen next? How is that character like or different from other characters in the story? Where does the story take place? Is there a problem? What is it? How is it solved? What have you learned?*

Do you know about SQ3R? It is a formula to help you understand what you read. It can be useful for any reading assignment. SQ3R is especially helpful when you are reading a textbook, like your social studies or science book. Each letter of the formula tells you what to do.

S = Survey

Survey means to look over the assignment. Look at the pictures. Look at the title and the headings, if there are any. Read the first sentence or two.

Q = Question

Question means to ask yourself, "What is this assignment about? What is the author trying to tell me?" Once you get an idea of what you are going to read, then you can read with a better understanding.

3R = Read, Recite, Review

1. Read the assignment, looking for the answers to the questions you had. Concentrate. Picture in your mind what the words are saying.

2. Recite in your mind, or write on paper, the main ideas of what you have just read. Write the main ideas in your own words.

3. Review what you have learned. Make notes to help you review.

Now you have a valuable study tool. Use it to help study for a test. Use it to help remember what you read. Use it to help understand important information.

Let's practice. Read the assignment on the next page. Use the SQ3R formula step by step.

Scholastic

Alexander Graham Bell invented the telephone. He was a teacher of the deaf in Boston. At night, he worked on experiments using a telegraph. Once when the metal in the telegraph stuck, Bell's assistant plucked the metal to loosen it. Bell, who was in another room, heard the sound in his receiver. He understood that the vibrations of the metal had traveled down the electric current to the receiver. He continued to work on this idea.

March 10, 1876, was the first time Alexander Graham Bell successfully spoke words over a telephone line. He was about to test a new transmitter when he spilled some battery acid on his clothes. He cried out to his assistant who was in another room, "Mr. Watson, come here! I want to see you!" Watson heard every word clearly on the telephone and rushed into the room.

Bell demonstrated his invention to many people. Over time, more and more telephone lines were installed, and people began to use the invention in their homes and businesses.

Did SQ3R help you? Let's find out.

1. Who invented the telephone? _____

2. What was his regular job? _____

3. What did Mr. Bell say to Mr. Watson during the first telephone conversation?

    _____

4. Who was Mr. Watson? _____

5. How did people first learn about the telephone? _____

    _____

Scholastic

*The **main idea** of a story tells what the story is mostly about. **Details** in a story tell more information about the main idea.*

What do you think of when you hear the words, "Milky Way"? Do you think of a candy bar? Well, there is another Milky Way, and you live in it! It is our galaxy. A galaxy is a grouping of stars. Scientists have learned that there are many galaxies in outer space. The Milky Way is a spiral-shaped galaxy with swirls of stars spinning out from the center of it. Some scientists believe there are hundreds of billions of stars in the Milky Way. One of those stars is the sun. Several planets orbit the sun. One of them is Earth. Even from Earth, on a clear night away from city lights, you can see part of the Milky Way. It is called that because so many stars close together look like a milky white stripe across the sky. However, if you looked at it with a telescope, you would see that it is made up of many, many stars.

Complete the main idea and each detail about the story.

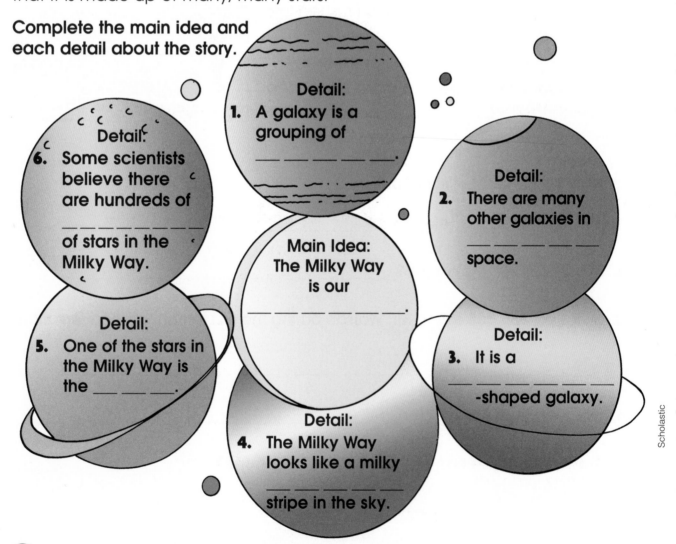

Detail:
1. A galaxy is a grouping of _ _ _ _ _ _.

Detail:
6. Some scientists believe there are hundreds of _ _ _ _ _ _ of stars in the Milky Way.

Detail:
2. There are many other galaxies in _ _ _ _ _ space.

Main Idea:
The Milky Way is our _ _ _ _ _ _ _ _.

Detail:
5. One of the stars in the Milky Way is the _ _ _.

Detail:
3. It is a _ _ _ _ _ _ -shaped galaxy.

Detail:
4. The Milky Way looks like a milky _ _ _ _ _ stripe in the sky.

Scholastic

Follow the directions to play each word game.

1. A palindrome is a word that is spelled the same forward or backward. Write each word backward. Circle each word that is a palindrome. Put an X on each word that is not.

wow _____

dad _____

mom _____

funny _____

noon _____

tall _____

deed _____

2. Some words imitate the noise that they stand for. For example, when you say "pop," it sounds like a popping sound! That is called "onomatopoeia." Unscramble each noise word. Write it correctly.

seechrc _____

owp _____

plurs _____

mobo _____

lckic _____

zzisel _____

chnucr _____

3. Homophones are words that sound alike when you say them but are spelled differently and have different meanings. For example, see and sea are homophones. Draw a line to match each pair of homophones.

knot   flew

break   soar

flu   not

sore   write

right   road

rode   brake

4. Add or subtract letters from each word to change it into another word. Write the new word.

peach – ch + r = _____

shirt – irt + oe = _____

sports – p – rts + ccer = _____

love – ove + ike = _____

chicken – c – ick = _____

brother – bro + nei = _____

Write your name and each of your classmates' names backward. Then pronounce each name. Are any of the names palidromes?

Scholastic

Berry Colorful Ink

 When sequencing a story, look for key words such as first, then, next, *and* finally *to help you determine the correct sequence.*

In early American schools, students used a quill pen and ink to practice writing letters and numerals. Since these schools did not have many supplies, the students often had to make their own ink at home. There were many different ways to make ink. One of the most common ways was to use berries such as blackberries, blueberries, cherries, elderberries, or strawberries. The type of berry used depended on the color of ink a student wanted. First, the type of berry to be used had to gathered. Then a strainer was filled with the berries and held over a bowl. Next, using the back of a wooden spoon, the berries were crushed. This caused the juice to strain into the bowl. After all the berry juice was strained into the bowl, salt and vinegar were added to the juice and then stirred. Finally, the juice was stored in a small jar with a tight-fitting lid. Not only did the students make colorful inks to use, they also made invisible and glow-in-the-dark inks.

Number the phrases below in the order given in the story.

_____ **The mixture was stirred.**

_____ **Using the back of a wooden spoon, the berries were crushed.**

_____ **The ink was stored in a small jar with a tight-fitting lid.**

_____ **Berries were gathered.**

_____ **All the berry juice was strained into the bowl.**

_____ **The strainer was held over a bowl.**

_____ **Salt and vinegar were added to the berry juice.**

_____ **A strainer was filled with berries.**

Scholastic

My Crazy Dream

I don't know why, but I went to school in my underwear. Everyone was laughing! I walked up and down the hall looking for my classroom, but I could never find it. Then I went to the Lost and Found box and put on some clothes. I heard my principal say, "Son, are you lost?" However, when I turned around, it was the President of the United States talking to me. He asked me to fly on his jet with him. As we were flying, I looked out the window and saw a pterodactyl flying next to us! How could that be? They are extinct! It smiled and waved good-bye. Then all of a sudden, the airplane turned into a roller coaster. It climbed upward a million miles, then down we went! For hours and hours we just kept going straight down! The roller coaster finally came to a stop, and I was on an island entirely made of chocolate. I ate a whole tree made of fudge! Then a native dressed in green feathers sneaked up behind me and captured me. He put me in a pot of boiling water to make soup out of me. I got hotter and hotter and hotter! Finally, I woke up and realized I had fallen asleep with my electric blanket on high.

Number the pictures in the order that they happened in the dream.

Scholastic

Have you ever wondered who invented potato chips? Some people say George Crum was the first person to make them . . . by accident! In 1853, he was a chef at an elegant restaurant in Saratoga Springs, New York, called Moon's Lake House. A regular item on the menu was fried potatoes, which was an idea that had started in France. At that time, French fried potatoes were cut into thick slices. One day, a dinner guest at Moon's Lake House sent his fried potatoes back to the chef because he did not like them so thick. So, Mr. Crum cut the potatoes a little thinner and fried them. The guest did not like those either. That made Mr. Crum angry, so he thought he would just show that guy. He sliced the potatoes paper-thin and fried them, thinking that would hush the complaining diner. However, his plan backfired on him! The diner loved the crispy, thin potatoes! Other diners tried them and also liked them. So, Mr. Crum's potato chips were added to the menu. They were called Saratoga Chips. Eventually, Mr. Crum opened his own restaurant to sell his famous chips. Now potato chips are packaged and sold in grocery stores worldwide!

Color each chip and its matching bag the same color.

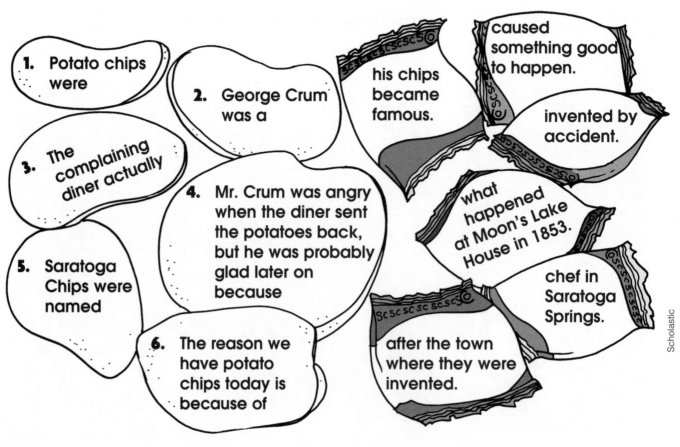

1. Potato chips were

2. George Crum was a

3. The complaining diner actually

4. Mr. Crum was angry when the diner sent the potatoes back, but he was probably glad later on because

5. Saratoga Chips were named

6. The reason we have potato chips today is because of

his chips became famous.

caused something good to happen.

invented by accident.

what happened at Moon's Lake House in 1853.

chef in Saratoga Springs.

after the town where they were invented.

Scholastic

Read each sentence. Use the other words in the sentence to figure out the meaning of the underlined word. Circle the word or phrase that means the same thing as the underlined word.

1. All of your hard work <u>merits</u> a day off of school. So you may stay home tomorrow.

    deserves   ruins   checks

2. When the sun came out, we took it as an <u>omen</u> that everything would be all right.

    dream   sign   wish

3. Please wash your <u>grubby</u> hands outside. They are covered with mud.

    dry   dirty   closed

4. The song sounded so beautiful when the choir started to sing in <u>unison</u>.

    poorly   at home   all together

5. You must <u>adapt</u> to our rules if you want to get along here.

    change   sing   react

6. I stayed in the sun too long and my skin was <u>scorched</u>.

    nice   cleaned   burned

7. The <u>hue</u> of her dress matched her skin perfectly.

    noise   color   belt

8. I tried to <u>conceal</u> my mess, but my mother found it anyway.

    hide   see   clean

Scholastic

Read each sentence. Use the other words in the sentence to figure out the meaning of the underlined word. Circle the word or phrase that means the same thing as the underlined word.

1. We have <u>ample</u> cookies for everyone. We may even have some left over.

too few   enough   no

2. Please <u>salvage</u> what you can so that you can give at least some of the work to your teacher.

hide   give away   save

3. When Todd won, his face became <u>radiant</u> with joy.

tearful   dull   gleaming

4. You must not <u>ponder</u> the question too long because you will not be able to finish the test.

think about   write   laugh at

5. This radio can <u>transmit</u> a message all the way to China.

send   destroy   drive

6. We climbed for days and finally reached the <u>zenith</u> of the mountain.

side   bottom   top

7. The <u>lame</u> bird had broken his wing and could not fly.

happy   injured   singing

8. Please <u>inflate</u> all of the balloons so that they will be nice and big.

blow up   pop   throw away

Scholastic

Making inferences *means to use information in a story to make judgments about information not given in the story.*

Read each riddle below. Look for clues to help you answer each question.

1. This thing keeps going faster and faster, up and down, and over and around. It tickles my tummy. The girls behind me are screaming. I hope I don't go flying out of my seat! Where am I?

_____

2. How will I ever decide? Look at all the different kinds. There are red hots, chocolates, candy corn, gummy worms, jawbreakers, and lollipops. Boy, this is my favorite place in the mall! Where am I?

_____

3. Let's sit in the front row! Ha ha ha! That's funny . . . a cartoon about a drink cup that is singing to a candy bar. That makes me hungry. I think I'll go get some popcorn before it starts. Where am I?

_____

4. I can see rivers and highways that look like tiny ribbons. I am glad I got to sit by the window. Wow, we are in a cloud! Yes, I would like a drink. Thank you. Where am I?

_____

5. Doctor, can you help my dog? His name is Champ. He was bitten by a snake, and his leg is swollen. I hope he will be all right. Where am I?

_____

Scholastic

The day we moved to our new house, there was a lot of work to do. Mom gave me the job of organizing the cabinets and closets. I unpacked each box and put things in their proper places. I filled up the medicine chest in the bathroom and the linen closet in the hall. I organized the silverware drawer in the kitchen, as well as the food in the pantry. I lined up Dad's stuff on the garage shelves. Last of all, I filled the bookshelf.

Write each word from the box in the correct category.

1. Medicine Chest

_____
_____
_____
_____

2. Linen Closet

_____
_____
_____
_____

3. Silverware Drawer

_____
_____
_____
_____

4. Pantry

_____
_____
_____
_____

5. Garage Shelves

_____
_____
_____
_____

6. Bookshelf

_____
_____
_____
_____

encyclopedias
eyedrops   teaspoons
car wax   motor oil
quilts   dictionary
cake mix   forks
serving spoons
atlas   aspirin
bandages   blankets
fishing tackle
crackers   novels
pillowcases
cereal   knives
sheets   toolbox
cough syrup
canned soup

THIS END UP

Scholastic

Facts *are true statement and can be proven.* **Opinions** *are a person's own personal views or beliefs.*

When people talk about things, they often mix news with opinions. Read each cartoon. Write *News* in the box if it is a fact. Write *Views* in the box if it is a person's own personal opinion.

1. **Punky Starr is the best rock singer that ever lived!**

2. **I like our new president. I think he is intelligent and kind.**

3. **Oranges were 3 for $1.00 at the Farmer's Market today.**

4. **Nobody likes me. Everyone thinks I am ugly.**

5. **When it gets dark, we will be able to see the Big Dipper and the North Star.**

6. **The city council will meet on Monday to vote on the new highway.**

7. **Ha ha ha ha! This show is funny.**

8. **The math homework for today is on page 34.**

9. **Your messy room looks like a pigpen!**

Scholastic

When you watch TV, you see a lot of commercials advertising different products. The people making the commercials want you to buy their product, so they make it sound as good as possible. Some of the things they say are facts, which can be proven. Other things are just the advertiser's opinion about how good the product is or how it will make you feel. Read each advertisement below. Write an *F* in the box beside each fact and an *O* in the box beside each opinion. The first one is done for you.

1.

Eat at Billy Bob's Burgers.

[O] best burgers in town

[F] made with 100% beef

2.

Drive an XJ-80 Sports Car today.

[ ] You'll never want to drive your old car again.

[ ] available in black, red, and silver

3.

[ ] You'll be the Coolest Kid on Your Block with a Pair of Xtreme In-Line Skates!

[ ] on sale for $79.99

4.

Sky-Diving Adventure Video Game

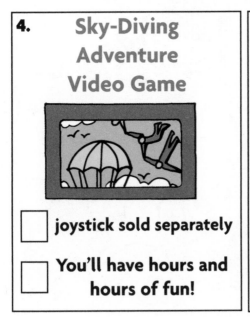

[ ] joystick sold separately

[ ] You'll have hours and hours of fun!

5.

Elastic Man, the Movie

[ ] full of heart-stopping action and mind-blowing special effects

[ ] "this year's best motion picture"

[ ] starring Academy-Award Winning Actor, Stretch Hamstring

[ ] now showing at the new Movie Town Theater

[ ] rated PG

Scholastic

There are three brothers who love to play sports. Each one is good at several different sports. Jeff plays hockey, football, soccer, and baseball. Allen plays hockey, football, tennis, and golf. Seth plays hockey, tennis, soccer, and basketball.

A. Complete the Venn diagram showing which sports each brother plays. Start with the sport all three brothers have in common. Write it in the shared space of all three circles.

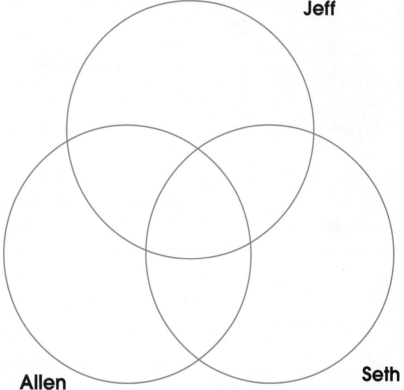

Jeff

Allen

Seth

B. Answer the questions.

1. What sport do all three boys like to play? _____

2. What sport do Jeff and Allen like to play that Seth does not? _____

3. What sport do Jeff and Seth like to play that Allen does not? _____

4. What sport do Allen and Seth like to play that Jeff does not? _____

5. What sport does Jeff like to play that no one else does? _____

6. What sport does Allen like to play that no one else does? _____

7. What sport does Seth like to play that no one else does? _____

Scholastic

Sharks

There are over 400 different kinds of sharks. The whale shark is the largest. It is as big as a whale. The dwarf lantern is the smallest. It is less than seven inches long.

All sharks live in the ocean, which is salt water, but a few kinds can swim from salt water to fresh water. Bull sharks have been found in the Mississippi River!

Sharks do not have bones. They have skeletons made of cartilage, which is the same thing your ears and nose are made of. A shark's skin is made of spiky, hard scales. The jaws of a shark are very powerful. When a great white shark bites, it clamps down on its prey and thrashes its head from side to side. It is the deadliest shark.

Sharks eat fish, dolphins, and seals. The tiger shark will eat just about anything. Some fishermen have discovered unopened cans of food, clocks, boat cushions, and even a keg of nails inside tiger sharks. Sometimes sharks even eat other sharks. For example, a tiger shark might eat a bull shark. The bull shark might have eaten a blacktip shark. The blacktip shark might have eaten a dogfish shark. So a tiger shark could be found with three sharks in its stomach!

Some sharks look very unusual. The hammerhead shark has a head shaped somewhat like a hammer, with eyes set very far apart. A cookie cutter shark has a circular set of teeth. When it bites a dolphin or whale, it leaves a perfectly round hole in its victim. The sawshark has a snout with sharp teeth on the outside, which makes it look like a saw. The goblin shark has a sharp-pointed spear coming out of its head, and its ragged teeth make it look scary!

The mako shark is the fastest swimmer. Sometimes makos have been known to leap out of the water, right into a boat! These are just a few of the many kinds of fascinating sharks.

Scholastic

Complete the chart with the name of the correct shark. If the statement is about all sharks, write *all*.

1. the largest shark	whale shark
2. the smallest shark	
3. the deadliest shark	
4. the fastest swimmer	
5. live in the ocean	
6. have skeletons of cartilage	
7. has a sharp-pointed spear coming out of its head	
8. has a head shaped like a hammer	
9. skin of spiky, hard scales	
10. leaves a round bite mark	
11. looks like a saw	
12. has eaten unopened cans, clocks, and boat cushions	

Scholastic

Best Friends

Amy dreaded recess every day. She did not have any friends to play with. All the girls in her class were paired up with a best friend or in groups, and she always felt left out. So, instead of playing with anyone, Amy just walked around by herself. She wanted to seesaw, but that is something you need to do with a friend. She liked to swing, but she could not go very high. She wished someone would push her to get her started.

One day, the teacher, Mrs. Gibbs, walked up and put her arm around Amy. "What's the matter, Amy? Why don't you play with the other children?" she asked kindly.

Amy replied, "Everyone has a friend except me. I don't have anyone." Mrs. Gibbs smiled and said, "Amy, the way to get a friend is to be a friend." Amy asked, "How do I do that?"

Mrs. Gibbs answered, "Look around the playground. There are three classes of third-graders out here during this recess time. Find someone who is alone and needs a friend. Then go to that person and ask them to play." Amy said she would think about it, but she was afraid she would be too embarrassed. She wasn't sure she could do it.

The next day, Amy noticed a dark-haired girl all alone on the playground. She worked up her courage and walked over to the girl. "Hi! My name is Amy. Do you want to play with me?" she asked.

"Okay," the girl said shyly. As they took turns pushing each other on the swings, Amy found out that the girl's name was Ming. She and her family had just moved from Japan. She did not know anyone and could not speak much English yet. She needed a friend.

"Want to seesaw?" Amy asked. Ming looked puzzled. Amy pointed to the seesaw. Ming smiled and nodded. Amy was so happy. She finally had a friend!

Scholastic

On each blank, write the letter of the picture that correctly answers the
question. One answer is used twice.

1. Where does this story take place? _____

2. Who is the main character in the story? _____

   Who are the other two characters in the story? _____ and _____

3. What is the problem in the story? _____

4. How does Amy solve her problem? _____

5. What is Ming's problem? _____

   How does Ming's problem get solved? _____

A.

Mrs. Gibbs

B.

playground

C.

Ming needed a friend, too.

D.

Ming

E.

Amy

F.

Amy asked Ming to play, and
they became friends.

G.

Amy needed a friend.

Scholastic

Earthquake!

*The **cause** in a story is what made something happen. The **effect** is what happened.*

Earthquakes are one of the most powerful events on the earth. When large sections of underground rock break and move suddenly, an earthquake occurs. This causes the ground to shake back and forth. Small earthquakes do not cause much damage, but large ones do. Some earthquakes have caused buildings and bridges to fall. Others have caused rivers to change their paths. Earthquakes near mountains and cliffs can cause landslides that cover up the houses and roads below. If a large earthquake occurs under the ocean, it can cause giant waves that flood the seashore. When large earthquakes occur in a city, there is danger of fire from broken gas lines and electric lines. Broken telephone lines and damaged roads make it difficult for rescue workers to help people who are in need. Scientists are trying to find ways to predict when an earthquake will happen so that people can be warned ahead of time.

Draw a shaky line under each effect.

Earthquakes can cause . . .
1. landslides
2. tornadoes
3. fires from broken gas and electric lines
4. huge waves that flood the seashore
5. swarms of flies
6. buildings and bridges to fall
7. sunburns
8. rivers to change their paths
9. damaged roads
10. lightning

Scholastic

Read the story and answer the questions.

There are so many ways to travel. The most common way to travel is probably in some type of motorized vehicle. If you are travelling with your family and you are not going far away, you could take a car. If you want to go somewhere with a lot of people, you could go in a van or bus. If you need to travel through the water, boats are another kind of transportation. We can go on small boats to travel to a close place. Big ships can take us to faraway lands. Submarines travel in the water also. They go way down deep into the water. Airplanes are also a great way to travel. Many people choose to fly in jet airplanes if they need to go far away and want to get there quickly. An airplane is fun to ride in because you can see the earth from way up high.

1. The main idea of this story is:
  a. there are many ways to travel.
  b. airplanes can go fast.
  c. you should just stay at home.

2. What type of transportation could you use to travel through the water?

_____

3. Why might someone choose to travel in an airplane?

_____

4. Where can big ships take us?

_____

5. Why is an airplane fun to ride in?

_____

6. What are five more ways that you can travel?

_____ _____ _____ _____ _____

Scholastic

Putting Men on the Moon

Have you ever heard of the "space race"? It sounds like a game, but it was not. The "space race" was a kind of contest between the United States and the Soviet Union. Both countries wanted to be the first to send people into outer space.

Both the Soviet Union and the United States sent rockets into space in the 1950s, but not people. Then in 1961, a man from the Soviet Union became the first person to travel in space. Yuri Gagarin went around Earth in a spaceship. He was in space for 108 minutes as he <u>orbited</u> Earth.

People in the United States were unhappy. They had hoped an American would be first in space. Soon President John F. Kennedy announced that Americans would be the first to land on the moon. He said they would get there by 1970.

Landing on the moon hardly seemed possible at the time. Only one American had ever traveled in space and for only 15 minutes. A trip to the moon and back would take eight days! But President Kennedy's promise was kept.

On July 16, 1969, a huge white rocket blasted off from the United States. It was carrying a spacecraft called *Apollo 11*. In the spacecraft were three U.S. astronauts: Neil Armstrong, Michael Collins, and Buzz Aldrin. They had been in training for many months. Now they were heading for the moon.

Apollo 11 traveled quickly through space. On the fourth day, it was near the moon. Armstrong and Aldrin put on spacesuits. They crawled into the *Eagle*. That was their landing craft. It would leave the command ship and land on the moon.

Collins stayed in the command ship. He orbited the moon while the *Eagle* went in for a landing. Armstrong and Aldrin watched the moon getting closer and closer. Finally Armstrong eased the landing craft down. He used his radio to tell people on Earth, "The *Eagle* has landed." He and Aldrin stepped out into a strange new world. They were walking on the moon!

Scholastic

1. Who was the first person to travel into space?
- Ⓐ Buzz Aldrin
- Ⓑ Neil Armstrong
- Ⓒ Michael Collins
- Ⓓ Yuri Gagarin

2. The article says, "He <u>orbited</u> Earth." What does <u>orbited</u> mean?
- Ⓕ went to
- Ⓖ left
- Ⓗ went around
- Ⓙ watched

3. Which men walked on the moon in 1969? Write their names.

_____

_____

4. Which of these things did Neil Armstrong do first?
- Ⓐ eased the *Eagle* down on the moon
- Ⓑ put on a spacesuit
- Ⓒ used his radio to talk to people on Earth
- Ⓓ crawled into the *Eagle*

5. Write a summary of *Apollo 11*'s trip to the moon.

_____

_____

_____

_____

Scholastic

"Poetry Play" Was a Great Success

Most of us had no idea what to expect last Monday. Our teachers told us that it was National Poetry Week. The whole school would be seeing a show called "Poetry Play."

When we got to the auditorium, we saw a big trunk in the middle of the stage. A man was sitting on it. After everyone sat down, the man stood up. He started pulling up the sail on a ship. There was no ship. There was no rope. He didn't say anything. But we could tell exactly what he was doing. We all got very quiet and watched. Soon he was sailing on the sea. He began speaking. "If I had a ship, I'd sail my ship." He was reciting "The Island," a poem by A. A. Milne.

By then we knew that Peter Williams, the man on stage, was going to give us a great performance. Between poems, he often lifted the lid of the trunk and stuck his head inside. When he came out, he had changed into a different character by putting on a funny nose or a hat. First he was a silly guy with big red cheeks and a round nose. Then he turned into a very proper English gentleman. Next he was a cat. With each change he used a different voice. Williams was truly amazing. He became five different characters and recited more than twenty poems in all.

His performance of "Jabberwocky" by Lewis Carroll was one of the best parts of the show. The poem is filled with made-up words. No one knows exactly what they mean. But when Peter Williams acted out the poem, it became an exciting adventure.

Williams was often very funny. But he was serious, too. He really showed how poems can fit every mood. He told us that we should say poems out loud. We should all try to learn some poems by heart. He left us with these words from a poem by Beatrice Shenk de Regniers: "Keep a poem in your pocket."

If you visit our school today, you'll see that Peter Williams's words came to life. In every room you will hear people reading poems out loud. Ask anyone what his or her favorite poem is. Your friend will probably start reciting it! "Poetry Play" got National Poetry Week off to a wonderful start.

Scholastic

1. The author's main purpose in writing this passage was to—
Ⓐ tell about a show called "Poetry Play."
Ⓑ explain how to write a poem.
Ⓒ make the reader want to learn poems by heart.
Ⓓ give information about poetry.

2. Which sentence tells an opinion?
Ⓕ Our teachers told us that it was National Poetry Week.
Ⓖ We saw a big trunk in the middle of the stage.
Ⓗ The poem is filled with made-up words.
Ⓙ "Poetry Play" got National Poetry Week off to a wonderful start.

3. Which sentence tells a fact?
Ⓐ "Poetry Play" was a great success.
Ⓑ He recited more than twenty poems.
Ⓒ His performance of "Jabberwocky" was one of the best parts of the show.
Ⓓ Williams was truly amazing.

4. Which of these is the title of a poem by A. A. Milne?
Ⓕ "Poetry Play"
Ⓖ "If I had a ship, I'd sail my ship"
Ⓗ "The Island"
Ⓙ "Jabberwocky"

5. What did Peter Williams do to change into a new character? Name two things.

_____

_____

6. Does this passage make you want to see "Poetry Play"? Tell why or why not.

_____

_____

Scholastic

The Lives of Turtles

There are about 270 kinds of turtles. Most turtles live near fresh water. They spend part of their time swimming in the water and part of it on land. Not all turtles live this way, though. Land turtles, also known as *tortoises*, do not swim at all. Sea turtles live nearly their whole lives in salt water.

Tortoises

Tortoises are slow and steady. They have short, thick back legs. Their flat front legs are built like shovels and are very good for digging. Tortoises have high, rounded shells, too. Many tortoises can pull their heads, legs, and tails inside their shells. They quickly do so at any sign of danger. Their strong shells protect them from animals that might want to eat them.

Turtles have no teeth. Instead they have strong beaks that can cut food like a pair of scissors. Unlike most other turtles, tortoises eat only plants.

Tortoises hatch from eggs. The female tortoise digs a hole, lays some eggs, and covers them with dirt. When the baby tortoises hatch, they must dig their way out of the hole. They never know their mother. The largest tortoises can grow to four feet long. They may weigh up to 600 pounds.

Sea Turtles

Like tortoises, sea turtles lay their eggs on land. The female turtle comes out of the ocean onto the beach. She digs a hole, lays her eggs, and returns to the sea. When the baby turtles hatch, they head straight for the water. The trip across the beach can be dangerous! Many animals come to the beach to eat the little turtles as they crawl toward the water. After they reach the water, male sea turtles never return to land. Females return only to lay their eggs.

Sea turtles can swim very fast. Their front legs are built like paddles. They use them like wings to "fly" through the water. Although most turtles can pull their heads and legs inside their shells, sea turtles cannot.

The green sea turtle eats only plants. Other sea turtles eat both plants and animals. The largest of all sea turtles is the leatherback. It can weigh over 1,000 pounds. Its favorite food is jellyfish.

Scholastic

1. Use what you learned in the article to label each picture. Which is the tortoise and which is the sea turtle?

 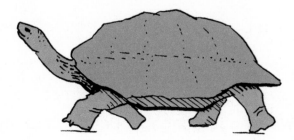

_____   _____

2. How are tortoises and sea turtles <u>alike</u>?
   Ⓐ Both eat animals.
   Ⓑ Both dig holes for their eggs.
   Ⓒ Both move slowly.
   Ⓓ Both have front legs that are good for digging.

3. How is the tortoise <u>different</u> from the sea turtle?
   Ⓕ The tortoise has a shell.
   Ⓖ It has no teeth.
   Ⓗ The tortoise hatches from an egg.
   Ⓙ It does not swim.

4. What is the largest kind of turtle, and how much does it weigh?

   _____

5. Which statement is true?
   Ⓐ Most turtles live near fresh water.
   Ⓑ Tortoises are the largest turtles.
   Ⓒ Most turtles live in the ocean.
   Ⓓ All turtles can pull their heads inside their shells.

Scholastic

Reading Skills & Reading Comprehension Practice Test

Fill in the bubble next to the correct answer.

1. Use the words in the sentence to figure out the meaning of the underlined word.

   We tried to <u>conceal</u> our plans but my sister found out about her surprise party anyway.

   ○ **A**　hide

   ○ **B**　forget

   ○ **C**　change

   ○ **D**　discover

2. Use the words in the sentence to figure out the meaning of the underlined word.

   She asked the children if they wanted ice cream and they answered "yes" in <u>unison</u>.

   ○ **F**　happily

   ○ **G**　slowly

   ○ **H**　all together

   ○ **J**　quietly

3. Which sentence comes FIRST in the story?

   ○ **A**　My tooth felt a lot better.

   ○ **B**　The dentist looked at my tooth.

   ○ **C**　My tooth hurt when I woke up.

   ○ **D**　My dad called the dentist.

Scholastic

Reading Skills & Reading Comprehension Practice Test

Read the story. Then fill in the bubble next to the correct answer.

Mom heard a faraway sound. "Help me!" cried Holly. Mom ran to the bathroom, but Holly was not there. She ran to the garage, but Holly was not there either. Finally, she ran to Holly's room and saw Holly's feet sticking out of the toy box, kicking wildly in the air!

4. What had happened to Holly?

○ **A**   She had fallen head first into the toy box and could not get out.

○ **B**   She was playing with blocks again.

○ **C**   She was playing hide-and-seek with Mom.

○ **D**   She was dancing with her friend.

Mom lifted Holly out of the box and asked, "Holly, are you all right?" Holly replied, "I think so." Holly then told Mom she had been looking for her toy piano because she wanted to play a song for her. "Do you want to hear the song now?" Holly asked. "First, let's have a special snack. You can play the piano for me later," Mom suggested. Holly thought that was a great idea!

5. Where was Holly's piano?

○ **F**   The piano was under Holly's bed.

○ **G**   The piano was at the bottom of the toy box.

○ **H**   It was in the closet.

○ **J**   It was behind the toy box.

Mom and Holly walked to the kitchen. Mom made Holly a bowl of ice cream with chocolate sauce and a cherry on top. Holly told Mom that she wanted to go to the park. Mom really liked that idea.

6. What will Mom and Holly do next?

○ **A**   They will go shopping.

○ **B**   They will go for a bike ride.

○ **C**   They will play on swings in the park.

○ **D**   Holly will play a song for Mom.

Scholastic

Reading Skills & Reading Comprehension Practice Test

Read each riddle. Look for clues to answer each question. Fill in the bubble next to the correct answer.

7. It is dark in here. I hear bats flying. With my flashlight, I see stalactites hanging above me. I hear water dripping. Where am I?

○ **A**   in a cave

○ **B**   at the movies

○ **C**   at a party

○ **D**   in the pool

8. I am all dressed up, sitting here quietly with my parents. The flowers are pretty. The music is starting. Here she comes down the aisle. I wish they would hurry so I could have some cake. Where am I?

○ **F**   at a party

○ **G**   at a wedding

○ **H**   at the zoo

○ **J**   at a play

9. This row has carrots growing, and this one onions. The corn is getting tall. The soil feels dry. I better water the plants today. Don't you think so, Mr. Scarecrow? Where am I?

○ **A**   in the garden

○ **B**   in my classroom

○ **C**   at the museum

○ **D**   at the planetarium

Scholastic

Choose a sticker to place here.

Fill in the bubble next to the correct answer.

10. Which item belongs in a box labeled School Supplies?

◯ **A**   grapes

◯ **B**   shirts

◯ **C**   pencils and pens

◯ **D**   goldfish

11. Which item belongs in a box labeled Medicine Chest?

◯ **F**   sheets

◯ **G**   forks

◯ **H**   motor oil

◯ **J**   cough syrup

12. Which item does NOT belong in a box labeled Books?

◯ **A**   dictionary

◯ **B**   bandages

◯ **C**   encyclopedias

◯ **D**   mystery novels

Scholastic

Vocabulary

Words! Words! Words! Words can do all kinds of things. They can show opposites. They may name people, places, and things. Words can describe things. They may come to us from other languages. Words may be made up of parts: root, prefix, suffix. They may sound silly! All of these things make words fun and interesting to learn!

The activities in this section introduce commonly used words and content area words that will become part of your child's growing vocabulary. Children who know lots of words become strong readers.

What to Do

Have your child complete the activity pages. Check his or her work. Cut out the Vocabulary Flash Cards on pages 137–141. Review them with your child throughout the year. Have your child make additional cards as he or she learns new words.

Keep On Going!

Have your child use the word cards to find antonyms, synonyms, homonyms, homophones, naming words, describing words, and so on. Also encourage your child to use the word cards to build sentences.

antonym

Synonym

Three of the four words in each group share something in common. Write what they have in common on the line. Then cross out the word that does not belong.

1.	wallet	gloves	socks	hat	_____
2.	adjective	comma	noun	verb	_____
3.	tornado	hurricane	earthquake	snow	_____
4.	square	sphere	pyramid	cube	_____
5.	Pacific	Europe	Antarctica	Asia	_____
6.	banana	apple	orange	peach	_____
7.	daffodil	oak	maple	elm	_____
8.	baseball	tennis	swimming	golf	_____
9.	delete	return	backspace	open	_____
10.	pupil	iris	cornea	palm	_____

Scholastic

A word can have different parts. Many words have a main part, or root. The root contains the basic meaning of the word. For example, ped is the root in the word pedal. The meaning of ped is "foot." Feet are used to push down on the pedals of a bicycle to cause it to move.

The root is missing from a word in each sentence below. Use context clues and the meaning of the roots in the box to figure out the missing word part. Then write it in the space to complete the word.

pos = place	**phon** = sound	**photo** = light
	port = carry	**pop** = people

1. The _____ulation of our town is just over 20,000.

2. The orchestra will perform a sym_____y by Beethoven next week.

3. The _____ition of the hour hand shows that it is 2:00 P.M.

4. What goods does our country ex_____ to other countries?

5. During _____synthesis, plants use sunlight to make food.

List the words you completed. Then write your own definition for each word. Use a dictionary if you are not sure.

6. _____

7. _____

8. _____

9. _____

10. _____

Scholastic

The prefix *un-* means either "not" or "do the opposite of" in each word below.
Circle each base word in the puzzle. The words go →, ←, ↑, ↓, ↗, and ↘.

unpack	untie	unwrap	unload	unlock	unfamiliar	unused
unwind	undo	unknown	unfold	unable	uncertain	unfair
uncover	unroll	unusual	unwise	unkind	unpainted	

R	A	I	L	I	M	A	F	X
N	E	E	O	F	F	O	L	D
I	S	E	A	W	A	X	L	E
A	I	X	D	L	I	I	O	T
T	W	K	N	O	W	N	R	N
R	E	V	O	C	Z	R	D	I
E	P	A	C	K	X	E	A	A
C	A	B	L	E	S	Y	Z	P
D	N	I	K	U	S	U	A	L

Write a word from the list to complete each sentence.

1. It is _____ for James to be late for school.

2. The name on the envelope was _____ to us.

3. It took me ten minutes to _____ the knot.

4. You need a key to _____ the trunk.

5. We grew more concerned as the story began to _____.

6. It is _____ to wait until the last minute to do your homework.

7. It took a week to _____ everything in the boxes after the move.

8. Bill thought the umpire's call was _____.

Scholastic

You can add a prefix to a root word to make a new word. Look at the list of prefixes, root words, and meanings below.

prefix	meaning	root word	meaning
de	away from	port	to carry
pre	before	dict	to say
circum	around	vent	to come
pro	forward	pos	to put
im	into		
contra	against		

For each word, fill in the meaning of the root word and prefix. Write a definition for each word.

1. deport

de _____ port _____

definition _____

_____

2. propose

pro _____ pose _____

definition _____

_____

3. predict

pre _____ dict _____

definition _____

_____

4. impose

im _____ pose _____

definition _____

_____

5. prevent

pre _____ vent _____

definition _____

_____

6. contradict

contra _____ dict _____

definition _____

_____

7. circumvent

circum _____ vent _____

definition _____

_____

8. import

im _____ port _____

definition _____

_____

Scholastic

You can add a prefix to a root word to make a new word. Look at the list of prefixes, root words, and meanings below.

prefix	meaning	prefix	meaning	root word	meaning
ab	away from	pre	before	rupt	to break
inter	between	pro	forward	ject	to throw
e	from			mit	to put
per	through			ceed	to go
trans	across			pel	to push
suc	up				

For each word, fill in the meaning of the root word and prefix. Write a definition for each word.

1. abrupt

ab _____ rupt _____

definition _____

_____

2. transmit

trans _____ mit _____

definition _____

_____

3. interject

inter _____ ject _____

definition _____

_____

4. succeed

suc _____ ceed _____

definition _____

_____

5. emit

e _____ mit _____

definition _____

_____

6. proceed

pro _____ ceed _____

definition _____

_____

7. permit

per _____ mit _____

definition _____

_____

8. propel

pro _____ pel _____

definition _____

_____

Scholastic

You can add a suffix to a root word to give a word a certain quality. Look at the list of suffixes, root words, and meanings below.

root word	meaning		suffix	meaning
anim	life		al	result of
cred	believe		ible	ability
vac	empty		ancy	a state of
annu	year		ive	a state of
act	to do		ist	a person
ver	true		age	activity
brev	short		ity	a state of

For each word, fill in the meaning of the root word and suffix. Write a definition for each word.

1. animal

anim _____ al _____

definition _____

_____

2. active

act _____ ive _____

definition _____

_____

3. credible

cred _____ ible _____

definition _____

_____

4. activist

act _____ ive _____ ist ___

definition _____

_____

5. vacancy

vac _____ ancy _____

definition _____

_____

6. verity

ver _____ ity _____

definition _____

_____

7. annual

annu _____ al _____

definition _____

_____

8. brevity

brev _____ ity _____

definition _____

_____

Scholastic

dove	record	live	lead	wind
dove	record	live	lead	wind

It rhymes with **love**.

A **dove** is a bird.

A **homograph** is a word that is spelled the same as another word but has a different meaning and sometimes a different pronunciation.

It rhymes with **stove**.

Dove is a past form of *dive*.

A band can **record** a song.
You can keep a **record** of your grades.

You **live** in a country.
A **live** flower is a living one.

Lead is a kind of metal.
If you **lead** a parade, you are at the beginning of it.

You must **wind** some clocks.
A strong **wind** can knock you down.

A. Read the words in each row. Circle three words that rhyme with the word at left.

1. live	hive	give	dive	five
2. lead	bead	head	bed	sled
3. dove	cove	drove	glove	rove
4. lead	bleed	feed	dead	weed
5. wind	find	grinned	hind	mind

B. Choose the correct word for each sentence. Write *a* or *b* in the blank.

a. rek′ ord   **b.** ree kord′

1. A thermometer will _____ the temperature.

2. The judge kept a _____ of the scores.

Scholastic

Say both pronunciations for each homograph. Then write the letter for the correct pronunciation for the homographs in the sentences. Use a dictionary if you are not sure of the meaning of a word.

refuse	a. (ref-yoos)	minute	a. (min-it)	close	a. (klohz)
	b. (ri-fyooz)		b. (mye-noot)		b. (klohss)
wound	a. (wound)	object	a. (ob-jikt)	sow	a. (sou)
	b. (woond)		b. (uhb-jekt)		b. (soh)

1. Give me a minute _____ to adjust the microscope, so you can clearly see the minute _____ germs.

2. The doctor cleaned the wound _____ on my arm and then wound _____ a bandage around it.

3. I refuse _____ to carry the refuse _____ to the Dumpster unless it is all in a sealed plastic bag.

4. Please close _____ the window that is close _____ to my desk.

5. The sow _____ ate the seeds as fast as I tried to sow _____ them.

6. Would you object _____ if I put this object _____ on your desk?

Scholastic

Homophones *are words that sound the same but are spelled differently and have different meanings.*

Write the correct homophone in each blank to complete the sentences.

1. **bored, board**
   Some of the _____ members seemed

   quite _____ at the last meeting.

2. **bare, bear**
   When a _____ cub is born, it is _____,
   and its eyes are closed.

3. **chilly, chili**
   Nothing tastes better than a bowl of _____ on a _____ day.

4. **raise, raze**
   Council members voted to _____ the buildings to make way for
   a new center, but they will have to _____ the money to build.

5. **guest, guessed**
   Who would have _____ that your _____ was a thief!

6. **patients, patience**
   I wonder if doctors ever lose their _____ with difficult
   _____ .

On another sheet of paper, rewrite each sentence using the correct homophones.

7. Aisle meat ewe at ate inn the mourning.

8. Would yew bee a deer and fix me sum tee and a boll of serial?

9. My ant and uncle lived oversees four too years in Madrid, the capitol city of Spain.

10. Alex was sick with the flue for fore daze and mist a hole weak of school.

11. I want two bye a knew pear of shoes, but I do not have a sent left.

12. Weed bettor put aweigh the pie before Harry eats it awl.

Scholastic

Homophones *are words that sound the same but are spelled differently and have different meanings.*

A. Read and write each word. Then group the homophones as partners.

 List Words

1. some _____   _____   _____

2. way _____   _____   _____

3. flower _____

4. close _____   _____   _____

5. hear _____   _____   _____

6. wood _____

7. flour _____   _____

8. would _____   _____

9. here _____

10. clothes _____

11. weigh _____

12. sum _____

🏆 **Challenge Words**

13. cookies _____

14. sugar _____

15. sprinkles _____

B. 👀 Write four list words that begin with two consonants.

_____   _____   _____   _____

Scholastic

A. Use a list word to complete each analogy.

1. *Spoon* is to *measure* as *scale* is to _____.

2. *Subtract* is to *difference* as *add* is to _____.

3. *Egg* is to *omelette* as _____ is to *cake*.

4. *Read* is to *book* as *wear* is to _____.

5. *Taste* is to *food* as _____ is to *sound*.

6. *Lose* is to *find* as *open* is to _____.

B. Circle the correct homophone to complete each sentence.

7. We find the (some, sum) by adding two numbers together.

8. The new (would, wood) furniture must (weigh, way) a ton!

9. The (flour, flower) has grown large (here, hear) in the sun.

10. Be sure to (close, clothes) the lid so the (flower, flour) will not spill.

11. (Would, Wood) you like to have some lemonade?

12. How did you find the (weigh, way) (here, hear)?

13. We will give (some, sum) old (close, clothes) to a charity.

C. Complete the puzzle using the challenge words.

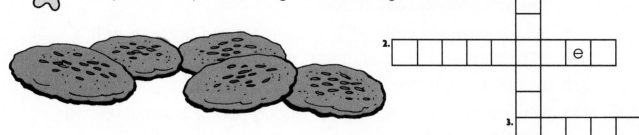

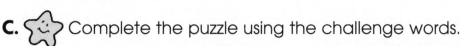

Words that have more than one meaning are called **homonyms**.

Read the words in the box.

stem	leaf	root	bark	trunk

What came to your mind when you read the words? Did you think of a tree? You may be surprised to know that the words are not just the names for parts of a tree.

Write a word from the box that matches both definitions.

1. _____
a. the sharp sound that a dog makes
b. the tough covering of a tree trunk and its branches

2. _____
c. plant part that grows from the stem and makes food
d. turn the pages

3. _____
e. stop the flow of something
f. the part of a plant that holds it up straight

4. _____
g. cheer for a team
h. the part of a plant that grows underground and takes in water and minerals from the soil

5. _____
i. the compartment of a car for storing a tire, baggage, and other items
j. the main stem of a tree

Write the missing word to complete each sentence. Then write the letter that tells the meaning of the word at the beginning of the sentence.

_____ **6.** The _____ was so enormous that it took 25 steps to walk around the tree.

_____ **7.** The beavers cut down the tree, ate the _____, and used the branches to build a dam.

_____ **8.** Which team did you _____ for, the Dodgers or the Yankees?

_____ **9.** By building a levee, the men could _____ the rising water.

_____ **10.** Why don't you _____ through book to see if you can identify the tree.

Scholastic

Antonyms *are words that have the opposite or nearly the opposite meanings.*

Write the antonym from the box for each word in ( ). Then decide which word is the better choice to complete the sentence. Write the missing word.

seldom	cheap	reduce	sharp	trust
public	group	absent	freeze	arrive

1. (present, _____) Megan has been _____ for two days because she has the flu.

2. (_____, expensive) The new computer game I want is so _____ that it will take months to save enough money to buy it.

3. (depart, _____) Be sure to check in at least two hours before your plane is scheduled to _____.

4. (_____, doubt) I do not _____ my memory, so I will write down the directions.

5. (melt, _____) Unless the temperature rises by 20 degrees, this ice will not _____).

6. (increase, _____) You had better _____ the heat, or you will burn the roast.

7. (_____, private) This is a _____ parking garage for apartment residents only.

8. (_____, often) We go to the shore so _____ that my parents decided to buy a beach house.

9. (individual, _____) Your toothbrush is for _____ use only.

10. (dull, _____) These scissors are only _____ enough to cut paper.

Scholastic

A **suffix** *is added to the end of a word to change its meaning. The suffix* -ous *means "having" or "full of."*

Write a word from the box that is the antonym of the clue word to complete the crossword puzzle.

tiny	silly	unclear	unknown	stingy	tasteless
calm	few	rude	careless	safe	timid

Across

1. delicious
4. anxious
5. numerous
6. courteous
10. enormous
11. cautious

Down

1. courageous
2. dangerous
3. generous
7. famous
8. serious
9. obvious

Scholastic

All the words in each group are supposed to be synonyms, but one word in each group belongs in one of the other groups. Cross out the word and write it in the correct group.

1. adult grown-up young mature _____	**2.** necessary powerful important required _____	**3.** slim slender skinny smart _____
4. chubby plump thin fat _____	**5.** pleasing agreeable lovely full-grown _____	**6.** empty huge gigantic vast _____
7. brave daring pleasant fearless _____	**8.** stuffed loaded packed needed _____	**9.** bare crowded vacant unfilled _____
10. bright bold intelligent clever _____	**11.** overweight mighty strong hardy _____	**12.** immature juvenile enormous undeveloped _____

Scholastic

Some words are not spelled the way they sound. Some words have silent consonants. Sometimes two or three consonants are blended together to make one sound.

Say each word. Notice how each beginning sound is spelled. Circle the letters making this sound. Then make a ✓ in the box that tells where each object may be seen. Use a dictionary to help.

1. knob
- ☐ on a door
- ☐ on a window
- ☐ on the floor

2. wrench
- ☐ in a refrigerator
- ☐ in a toolbox
- ☐ in a sewing kit

3. cello
- ☐ at a grocery store
- ☐ at a post office
- ☐ in an orchestra

4. photograph
- ☐ on a CD player
- ☐ in a garden
- ☐ in an album

5. schedule
- ☐ in a classroom
- ☐ in a music book
- ☐ in a cookbook

6. gnu
- ☐ at a museum
- ☐ in an office
- ☐ at a zoo

7. wren
- ☐ in a jewelry box
- ☐ at a bird feeder
- ☐ on a workbench

8. gnome
- ☐ in the garage
- ☐ in the attic
- ☐ in a fairy tale

9. knuckle
- ☐ in your lunchbox
- ☐ in your body
- ☐ in your book bag

10. knickknack
- ☐ on a shelf
- ☐ in a freezer
- ☐ in a closet

11. ghost
- ☐ in a dishwasher
- ☐ in the sea
- ☐ in a scary movie

12. xylophone
- ☐ in a marching band
- ☐ in a kitchen
- ☐ on a desk

 Think of words that end with *lf* **as in** *calf* **and** *lk* **as in** *talk.* **Which letter is silent?**

Scholastic

A **compound word** *is made up of two smaller words whose definitions give meaning to the new word.*

A. How many compound words can you make? Write as many as you can by putting together two words. If needed, use another sheet of paper.

school	side	water	room	time
back	under	light	store	break
fall	house	proof	down	ground
wood	town	foot	work	print
door	fire	step	out	mean

_____   _____   _____   _____

_____   _____   _____   _____

_____   _____   _____   _____

_____   _____   _____   _____

_____   _____   _____   _____

_____   _____   _____   _____

_____   _____   _____   _____

B. Complete each sentence with a compound word that can be made with two words above.

1. I made a _____ of the information I found online.

2. The wallpaper has yellow flowers on a white _____.

3. A raincoat should be _____.

4. We live in a two-story _____.

5. That dance requires some very fancy _____!

Scholastic

A **compound word** *is made up of two smaller words whose definitions give meaning to the new word.*

A. Read and write each word. Then separate each compound into two smaller words.

List Words

1. springtime _____ _____ _____

2. someone _____ _____ _____

3. birthday _____ _____ _____

4. afternoon _____ _____ _____

5. outdoors _____ _____ _____

6. everything _____ _____ _____

7. homework _____ _____ _____

8. skateboard _____ _____ _____

9. notebook _____ _____ _____

10. breakfast _____ _____ _____

11. bluebird _____ _____ _____

12. upstairs _____ _____ _____

Challenge Words

13. butterfly _____

14. grasshopper _____

15. ladybug _____

B. Write four list words that begin with vowels.

_____ _____ _____ _____

Scholastic

A. Use list words to complete the story.

  Cody raced through the door and threw his books down. The warm air outside told him that _____ had finally arrived. He could not wait to get _____, but he knew he would have to finish his _____ first. He ran _____ to his bedroom and grabbed a pencil and _____ from his desk. He sat down to write his story, but he could not think of a good topic. Just then, a _____ landed on his window ledge. "That's it!" Cody shouted. He finished his story in no time and ran outside to jump on his new _____. "I love springtime!" he shouted.

B. Match the words to create compound list words. Write them on the lines.

home	fast	bird	_____	_____
board	up	break	_____	_____
stairs	skate	blue	_____	_____
note	book	work		

_____   _____   thing   some   birth

_____   _____   one   doors   every

_____   _____   after   out   noon

                 day   time   spring

C. Label each insect picture using a challenge word.

Scholastic

Read each sentence and the question that follows. Then write the correct word to answer the question. Use a dictionary if you are unfamiliar with the meaning of a word.

1. You read the first copy of an author's book.
   Did you read the first <u>addition</u> or <u>edition</u>? _____

2. You make a list of everything you need.
   Are you <u>through</u> or <u>thorough</u>? _____

3. You swing the bat and miss a third time.
   Is it the <u>empire</u> or <u>umpire</u> who yells, "You're out!"? _____

4. You are dressed like a clown for the party.
   Are you wearing a <u>custom</u> or <u>costume</u>? _____

5. You get up early without waking anyone else.
   Are you <u>quiet</u>, <u>quite</u>, or <u>quit</u>? _____

6. You read a book about Tony Hawk.
   Is it a <u>bibliography</u> or a <u>biography</u>? _____

7. Your teacher said you did an excellent job on your report.
   Did your teacher <u>command</u> or <u>commend</u> you? _____

8. You chop celery into tiny pieces for the egg salad.
   Is the celery <u>finally</u> or <u>finely</u> chopped? _____

9. You are 48 inches tall. Your best friend is 46 inches tall.
   Are you taller <u>then</u> or <u>than</u> your friend? _____

10. You multiplied the base times the height of a rectangle.
    Did you find the <u>aria</u> or <u>area</u> of the shape? _____

Scholastic

Some words are confusing because they are similar in some way.

Read each sentence and question. Decide which underlined word correctly answers the question. Then write the word.

1. A package just arrived for Jason. Did he <u>accept</u> it or did he <u>except</u> it? _____	**2.** Sam had a sundae after dinner. Did he have <u>desert</u> or <u>dessert</u>? _____
3. Beth made a right triangle. Does it have three <u>angels</u> or <u>angles</u>? _____	**4.** All the actors sang and danced the last number. Did they perform the <u>finale</u> or the <u>finally</u>? _____
5. Megan swam the length of the pool underwater. Did she hold her <u>breathe</u> or her <u>breath</u>? _____	**6.** Aaron's socks slid down to his ankles. Were they <u>loose</u> or <u>lose</u>? _____
7. Jerome just made a dental appointment. Should he mark it on the <u>colander</u> or the <u>calendar</u>? _____	**8.** Lisa opened the gate and watched as the cows ate grass. Are the cows out to <u>pastor</u> or <u>pasture</u>? _____
9. Meg addressed an envelope. Should she add a <u>coma</u> or <u>comma</u> between the town and state? _____	**10.** Anna sketched a scene from a story she just read. Did she draw a <u>pitcher</u> or a <u>picture</u>? _____

 Are there any words that confuse you? Record them in a notebook. Include the definition and a sentence using the word. Think of ways to help yourself remember confusing words.

Scholastic

Many everyday words in English are words from other languages.

Write the language from which you think each word comes. Then use a dictionary to find out if you are correct. Here is an example of an entry for sauerkraut.

sauerkraut \\'saŭ(-ə)r-ˌkraŭt\ *n* a German dish of shredded cabbage that has been salted and allowed to sour. (1617) [German, "sour greens."]

African	Chinese	Dutch	Russian
Spanish	German	Arabic	Turkish
Yiddish	Japanese	Italian	French

	Guess	Check
1. hamburger	_____	_____
2. banjo	_____	_____
3. tea	_____	_____
4. cookie	_____	_____
5. yogurt	_____	_____
6. piano	_____	_____
7. parka	_____	_____
8. chocolate	_____	_____
9. chef	_____	_____
10. bagel	_____	_____
11. magazine	_____	_____
12. karate	_____	_____

Scholastic

Read the words in each category. Think about how they are related. Then select and write a word or phrase from the box that best completes the title of each category.

Government	Oceans	Inventors	States
National Symbols	Leaders	Landforms	Map
Mountain Ranges	Nations	Explorers	Cities

Names of _____ California New Jersey Louisiana	Examples of _____ Bald eagle Liberty Bell "Stars and Stripes"	Names of _____ Alexander Graham Bell Philo Farnsworth Thomas Edison
Kinds of _____ plateau mountain valley	Kinds of _____ mayor governor president	Names of _____ New Zealand Brazil Egypt
Names of _____ Hernando Cortes Henry Hudson Christopher Columbus	Parts of a _____ lines of latitude distance scale compass rose	Branches of _____ Legislative Judicial Executive
Names of _____ Rockies Sierra Nevada Appalachian	Names of _____ Baltimore Orlando San Francisco	Names of _____ Arctic Indian Pacific

Scholastic

Many words have been shortened or clipped over time. Write the shortened form of each word. Then circle the shortened form in the puzzle below. The words go ←, →, ↑, ↓, ↖, ↘, and ↗.

laboratory = _____

champion = _____

referee = _____

bicycle = _____

veterinarian = _____

gasoline = _____

examination = _____

airplane = _____

telephone = _____

mathematics = _____

stereophonic = _____

moving picture = _____

refrigerator = _____

advertisement = _____

submarine = _____

automobile = _____

photograph = _____

facsimile = _____

teenager = _____

taxicab = _____

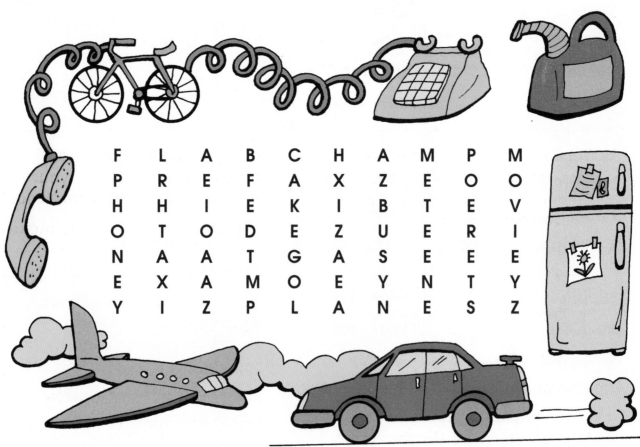

```
F   L   A   B   C   H   A   M   P   M
P   R   E   F   A   X   Z   E   O   O
H   H   I   E   K   I   B   T   O   V
O   T   O   D   E   Z   U   E   R   I
N   A   A   T   G   A   S   E   E   E
E   X   A   M   O   E   Y   N   T   Y
Y   I   Z   P   L   A   N   E   S   Z
```

Scholastic

Look at the diagram. Then read the clues and use the words to complete the crossword puzzle.

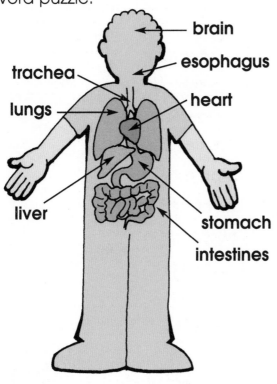

brain

esophagus

trachea

heart

lungs

liver

stomach

intestines

Across

2. Your _____ are the part of the respiratory system that help bring air into your body and get rid of carbon dioxide.

5. Your small and large _____ are the parts of the digestive system that break down food into nutrients and then eliminate waste.

6. Your _____ pumps blood throughout your body.

7. When you inhale, air passes through your _____ to your lungs.

Down

1. Your _____ is the part of your nervous system that tells your muscles and organs what to do.

2. One job of your _____ is to make bile to help break down food in your small intestine.

3. Your _____ is the part of your digestive system where a powerful acid breaks down the food you have just swallowed.

4. After you chew and swallow, food passes through your _____ to your stomach.

Scholastic

There are many terms related to music that are important to know.

percussion	harmony	opera	jazz
rhythm	woodwind	soprano	melody
composer	conductor	musician	orchestra
brass	string	keyboard	tenor

Write the correct word for each clue. Then write the letter from the boxes in order on the line below to answer the musical question.

1. one who sings or plays a musical instrument

   _ _ ☐ _ _ _ _ _

2. the main tune of a musical piece

   _ _ _ _ _ _ ☐

3. one who writes music

   _ _ ☐ _ _ _ _ _

4. a play that is sung to music

   _ ☐ _ _ _

5. large group of performers who play classical music

   _ _ _ ☐ _ _ _ _

6. an instrument such as a flute, oboe, or bassoon

   _ _ ☐ _ _ _

7. one who directs a musical group

   _ _ ☐ _ _ _ _ _

8. pattern of beats in music

   _ _ ☐ _ _ _

What do you call a musical work written for an orchestra? _____

Scholastic

Write the word from the box that correctly completes each analogy.

south	continent
inventor	resolution
nation	immigrant
state	demand
elect	consumer
century	communication

1. *Abraham Lincoln* is to *president* as *Thomas Edison* is to _____.

2. *Dime* is to *dollar* as *decade* is to _____.

3. *Mexico* is to *country* as *North America* is to _____.

4. *Railroad* is to *transportation* as *telegraph* is to _____.

5. *East* is to *west* as *north* is to _____.

6. *Mayor* is to *town* as *governor* is to _____.

7. *Colony* is to *settlement* as *country* is to _____.

8. *Problem* is to *solution* as *producer* is to _____.

9. *Import* is to *export* as *supply* is to _____.

10. *Barter* is to *trade* as *choose* is to _____.

11. *War* is to *peace* as *conflict* is to _____.

12. *Majority* is to *minority* as *native* is to _____.

 Write the number of analogies that are antonyms. _____

Scholastic

Fill in the circle next to the phrase that correctly completes each analogy.

1. *Plumber* is to *pipes* as

    ○ *librarian* is to *library.*   ○ *mechanic* is to *cars.*

2. *Degree* is to *thermometer* as

    ○ *ruler* is to *measurement.*   ○ *kilogram* is to *scale.*

3. *Student* is to *teacher* as

    ○ *patient* is to *physician.*   ○ *courtroom* is to *lawyer.*

4. *Sweet* is to *sour* as

    ○ *cup* is to *mug.*   ○ *lost* is to *found.*

5. *Gymnasium* is to *gym* as

    ○ *gasoline* is to *gas.*   ○ *photograph* is to *photographer.*

6. *Wade* is to *weighed* as

    ○ *fiction* is to *fact.*   ○ *borough* is to *burrow.*

7. *Centimeter* is to *cm* as

    ○ *gram* is to *g*   ○ *January* is to *month.*

8. *Blue whale* is to *krill* as

    ○ *elephant* is to *mammal.*   ○ *koala* is to eucalyptus *leaves.*

9. *Repair* is to *destroy* as

    ○ *hire* is to *fire.*   ○ *depart* is to *leave.*

10. *Bronco* is to *Spanish* as

    ○ *language* is to *Latin.*   ○ *spaghetti* is to *Italian.*

Scholastic

population	intelligent
position	hardy
photosynthesis	enormous
pleasing	strong
stuffed	mighty
loaded	uncover
crowded	unable
clever	uncertain

photographer	credible
spaghetti	active
thermometer	annual
deport	extraction
impose	record
prevent	live
propose	lead
circumvent	bark

leaf	knuckle
reduce	wrench
expensive	knickknack
cheap	wallpaper
stingy	underwater
generous	quiet
delicious	quite
famous	quit

Vocabulary Practice Test

Fill in the bubble next to the correct answer.

1. Which word does NOT belong in the group?
   - A pencil
   - B crayons
   - C markers
   - D book

2. Which word does NOT belong in the group?
   - F circle
   - G square
   - H cube
   - J rectangle

3. Which word is the shorter form of advertisement?
   - A ad
   - B add
   - C adtise
   - D advert

Scholastic

Vocabulary Practice Test

Fill in the bubble next to the correct answer.

4. Which word has to do with light?

○ **A**   population

○ **B**   photograph

○ **C**   phonograph

○ **D**   deport

5. Which word has both a prefix and a suffix?

○ **F**   submit

○ **G**   submitting

○ **H**   extract

○ **J**   multiply

6. Which word is NOT a compound word?

○ **A**   raincoat

○ **B**   townhouse

○ **C**   workout

○ **D**   grounded

Scholastic

Grammar/Writing

To be successful at playing any game, you have to understand the rules. The same thing is true of writing. Grammar provides the rules your child needs to become a successful writer.

The activities in this section set out the rules for writing. They start with the four types of sentences and the punctuation for each. Familiarity with these is crucial to good writing. Your child will also learn the parts of speech: nouns, pronouns, adjectives, and verbs, and how to use them to build clear, interesting, and well-developed sentences.

What to Do
Each new skill starts with a definition or explanation. Have your child read the definitions or explanations on the activity page. Then have your child complete the activity. Review his or her work together. Let your child know that he or she is doing a great job!

Keep On Going!
Make learning grammar fun! Take a walk together. On your walk, play a game with your child. See who can name the greatest number of naming words they see around the neighborhood: trees, flowers, houses, Mrs. Jackson, and so on. Challenge each other to come up with the greatest number of words to describe the things you see on your walk: The huge, green, pine tree, full of pointy, brown pine-cones is next to the delicate, bright pink azalea bush.

A **sentence** is a group of words that expresses a complete thought.
A **fragment** is an incomplete thought.

Write *S* for sentence or *F* for fragment.

_____ **1.** Insects eat many different things.

_____ **2.** Some of these things.

_____ **3.** The praying mantis eats other insects.

_____ **4.** Water bugs eat tadpoles and small frogs.

_____ **5.** Flower nectar makes good.

_____ **6.** Build nests to store their food.

_____ **7.** The cockroach will eat almost anything.

_____ **8.** Termites.

_____ **9.** A butterfly caterpillar.

_____ **10.** Bite animals and people.

_____ **11.** Some insects will even eat paper.

_____ **12.** Insects have different mouth parts to help

them eat.

Scholastic

*A **statement** is a sentence that tells something. It ends with a period. A **question** is a sentence that asks something. It ends with a question mark.*

A. Read each sentence. Write *Q* on the line if the sentence is a question. Write *S* if the sentence is a statement.

1.   Where did the ant live?   ———————

2.   The ant had many cousins.   ———————

3.   She found the crumb under a leaf.   ———————

4.   How will she carry it?   ———————

5.   Who came along first?   ———————

6.   The lizard wouldn't help.   ———————

7.   He said he was too cold.   ———————

8.   Why did the rooster fly away?   ———————

B. The sentences below do not make sense. Rewrite the words in the correct order.

1.   How crumb did carry the ant the?   _____

_____

2.   She herself it carried.

_____

_____

Scholastic

*An **exclamation** is a sentence that shows strong feeling. It ends with an exclamation
point. A **command** is a sentence that gives an order. It ends with a period.*

A. Read each sentence. Write *E* on the line if the sentence is an
exclamation. Write *C* if the sentence is a command.

1.   They chase buffaloes!   ———

2.   You have to go, too.   ———

3.   Wait at the airport.   ———

4.   It snows all the time!   ———

5.   Alligators live in the sewers!   ———

6.   Look at the horse.   ———

7.   That's a great-looking horse!   ———

8.   Write a letter to Seymour.   ———

B. Complete each exclamation and command. The punctuation mark at
the end of each line is a clue.

1.   I feel ————————————————————————————————!

2.   Help your ——————————————————————————————.

3.   That's a ———————————————————————————————!

4.   I lost —————————————————————————————————!

5.   Turn the ———————————————————————————————.

6.   Come watch the —————————————————————————.

7.   Please let me ———————————————————————————.

Scholastic

*The **simple subject** is the main word in the complete subject. The **simple predicate** is the main word in the complete predicate.*

A. Read each sentence. Draw a line between the complete subject and the complete predicate. Then write the simple subject and the simple predicate.

	Simple Subject	Simple Predicate
1. Mrs. Perez's class took a trip to the museum.	_____	_____
2. Many large paintings hung on the walls.	_____	_____
3. Maria saw a painting of an animal alphabet.	_____	_____
4. All the children looked at the painting.	_____	_____
5. Paul pointed to a cat on a leash.	_____	_____
6. His friend liked the dancing zebra.	_____	_____
7. Everyone laughed at the purple cow.	_____	_____
8. Many people visited the museum that day.	_____	_____
9. The bus took us to school.	_____	_____

B. Finish the sentences. Add a complete subject to sentence 1.
Add a complete predicate to sentence 2.

1. _____ was funny.

2. My class _____.

Scholastic

*A **compound subject** is two or more nouns connected by **and**. A **compound predicate** is two or more verbs connected by **and**.*

A. Underline the compound subject or the compound predicate in each sentence. Write *CS* above each compound subject and *CP* above each compound predicate.

1. Mike and Jody moved away.

2. They often call and e-mail us.

3. Mike jogs and swims every day.

4. Phil and Jan will visit them.

5. Juan and Yoshi moved here from other countries.

6. They speak and read English very well.

7. Lori, Sam, and Beth wrote a play about moving.

8. They practiced and presented it to the class.

9. We clapped and smiled at the end.

10. The parents and the principal liked the play.

B. Complete one sentence with the compound subject. Complete the other sentence with the compound predicate.

My dad and sister   barked and jumped

1. Buster ————————————————— when we got home.

2. ————————————————— played word games for an hour.

Scholastic

*A **singular noun** names one person, place, or thing. A **plural noun** names more than one person, place, or thing. Add **-s** to form the plural of most nouns.*

A. Each sentence has an underlined noun. On the line, write *S* if it is a singular noun. Write *P* if it is a plural noun.

1. She has a new <u>baby</u>. ————

2. <u>She</u> is very cute. ————

3. She has small <u>fingers</u>. ————

4. She drinks from a <u>bottle</u>. ————

5. I can tell my <u>friends</u> all about it. ————

B. Read each sentence. Underline the singular noun. Circle the plural noun.

1. The baby has two sisters.

2. The nightgown has pockets.

3. Her hand has tiny fingers.

4. My parents have a baby.

5. The family has three girls.

C. Complete the chart. Write the singular or plural of each noun.

Singular	Plural
fence	
	trains
gate	
	cows

Scholastic

A **common noun** *names any person, place, or thing.* A **proper noun** *names a particular person, place, or thing. A proper noun begins with a capital letter.*

A. Read each word in the box. Write it where it belongs on the chart.

doctor	park	football	Tangram	Pat	Atlanta

Category	Common Nouns	Proper Nouns
1. **Person**		
2. **Place**		
3. **Thing**		

B. Complete each sentence with a common noun or proper noun. In the box, write *C* if you wrote a common noun. Write *P* if you wrote a proper noun.

1. I threw the ball to ———————————. (person) ☐

2. I have visited ———————————. (place) ☐

3. My favorite food is ———————————. (thing) ☐

4. My family lives in ———————————. (place) ☐

5. My favorite author is ———————————. (person) ☐

6. I wish I had a ———————————. (thing) ☐

7. I like to read about ———————————. (historical event) ☐

8. My favorite holiday is ———————————. (holiday) ☐

Scholastic

*A **possessive noun** shows ownership. Add **'s** to make a singular noun show ownership. Add an apostrophe (') after the **s** of a plural noun to show ownership.*

A. Underline the possessive noun in each sentence. Write *S* on the line if the possessive noun is singular. Write *P* if the possessive noun is plural.

1. Anna's family took a walk in the woods.   ————

2. They saw two birds' nests high up in a tree.   ————

3. A yellow butterfly landed on Brad's backpack.   ————

4. Anna liked the pattern of the butterfly's wings.   ————

5. A turtle's shell had many spots.   ————

6. Anna took pictures of two chipmunks' homes.   ————

7. The animals' tails had dark stripes.   ————

B. Complete each sentence with the singular possessive form of the noun in ( ).

1. Jim was going to play basketball at ——————— house. (Carol)

2. One of ——————— new sneakers was missing. (Jim)

3. He looked under his ——————— desk. (sister)

4. He crawled under his ——————— bed to look. (brother)

5. It was outside in his ——————— flower garden. (dad)

6. The ——————— lace had been chewed. (sneaker)

7. Jim saw his ——————— footprints in the dirt. (dog)

Scholastic

⟹ *A **singular pronoun** takes the place of a noun that names one person, place, or thing. A **plural pronoun** takes the place of a noun that names more than one person, place, or thing.*

A. Underline the pronoun in each sentence. On the line, write *S* if it is singular or *P* if it is plural.

1. He is called Spider. _____

2. I can see Spider has eight long legs. _____

3. They asked Spider a question. _____

4. We want to know what's in the pot. _____

5. It contains all the wisdom in the world. _____

B. Read each pair of sentences. Circle the pronoun in the second sentence. Then underline the word or words in the first sentence that it replaces. Write the pronoun under *Singular* or *Plural*.

	Singular	**Plural**
1. This story is funny. It is about wisdom.	_____	_____
2. The author retold the story. She is a good writer.	_____	_____
3. My friends and I read the story aloud. We enjoyed the ending.	_____	_____
4. Two boys acted out a scene. They each took a different role.	_____	_____

C. For each noun write a subject pronoun that could take its place.

1. Spider _____

2. the pot _____

3. Tortoise and Hare _____

4. Spider's mother _____

Scholastic

A **pronoun** *takes the place of a noun or nouns in a sentence. The words* **me, you, him, her, it, us,** *and* **them** *are object pronouns. Use these object pronouns in the predicates of sentences.*

A. Underline the object pronoun in each sentence.

1. Aunt Cindy gave us a football.

2. Our dog Rex found it.

3. He thinks the ball is for him.

4. I said, "Rex, that's not for you!"

5. Aunt Cindy gave me another ball for Rex.

6. Now Rex always wants to play with her.

7. I like to watch them.

B. Decide which object pronoun below can replace the underlined word or words. Write the object pronoun on the line.

1. I went to the movies with <u>Rachel and Kevin</u>. _____

2. Kevin asked <u>Rachel</u> for some popcorn. _____

3. Rachel was happy to share <u>the popcorn</u>. _____

4. I accidentally bumped <u>Kevin</u>. _____

5. The popcorn spilled all over <u>Rachel, Kevin, and me</u>. _____

C. Write two sentences. In one sentence use a subject pronoun.
In the other sentence use an object pronoun.

1. _____

2. _____

Scholastic

A **possessive pronoun** *shows ownership or belonging. It takes the place of a noun that shows ownership.* **My, your, his, her, its, our,** *and* **their** *are possessive pronouns.*

A. Circle the subject pronoun in each sentence. Then underline the possessive pronoun. Use these answers to fill in the chart. The first one has been done for you.

1. I am planning a trip with my family.

2. Will you wear your sunglasses?

3. He will bring his camera.

4. She will take her dog along.

5. It will eat all its food.

6. We will enjoy our vacation.

7. They will show their pictures.

Subject Pronouns	Possessive Pronouns
I	my
_____	_____
_____	_____
_____	_____
_____	_____
_____	_____
_____	_____

B. Underline the possessive pronoun in each sentence.

1. The desert is their home.

2. Her umbrella blocks out the sun.

3. That javelina likes to play his guitar.

4. His address is 1 Tumbleweed Avenue.

5. Coyote said, "My stomach is growling."

6. "I'll blow your house down," Coyote shouted.

7. Its walls are made of tumbleweeds.

8. "Our house is strong," the third Javelina said.

Scholastic

Action verbs *are words that tell what the subject of the sentence does.*

A. Underline the action verb in each sentence.

1. The villagers cheered loudly.

2. They added flavor to the cheese.

3. Please give them the milk.

4. He serves the cheese.

5. He emptied the buckets.

B. Circle the action verb in ( ) that paints a more vivid picture of what the subject is doing.

1. The villagers (walked, paraded) across the floor.

2. Father (whispered, talked) to the baby.

3. The puppy (ate, gobbled) down his food.

4. The girl (skipped, went) to her chair.

5. The ball (fell, bounced) down the stairs.

C. Write an action verb from the box to complete each sentence.

| whispered | laughed | sighed |

1. We _____ at the playful kittens.

2. She _____ deeply and fell asleep.

3. Megan _____ to her friend in the library.

Scholastic

Present-tense verbs *must agree in number with the subject. The letters* **-s** *or* **-es** *are usually added to a present-tense verb when the subject of the sentence is a singular noun or* **he, she,** *or* **it**.

A. Read each sentence. On the line, write the correct form of the present-tense verb in ( ).

1. The crow ———————— the pitcher with pebbles. (fill, fills)

2. The man ———————— the crow. (watch, watches)

3. Then he ———————— the cabbage across the river. (take, takes)

4. The man and the goat ———————— the wolf behind. (leave, leaves)

5. They ———————— back on the last trip. (go, goes)

B. Write the correct past-tense form of the verb in ( ).

1. J.J. ———————— for the hidden picture. (look)

2. He ———————— at it for a long time. (stare)

3. Ana ———————— by. (walk)

4. Then she ———————— solve the puzzle. (help)

C. Write three sentences. Use the verb in ( ) in your sentence.

1. (play) ————————————————————————

————————————————————————————————

2. (plays)————————————————————————

————————————————————————————————

3. (played) ———————————————————————

————————————————————————————————

Scholastic

The verb **to be** *tells what the subject of a sentence is or was.* **Am, is,** *and* **are** *tell about someone or something in the present.* **Was** *and* **were** *tell about someone or something in the past.*

A. Read each sentence. Circle the word that is a form of the verb *to be*.

1. Captain Fossy was Mr. Anning's good friend.

2. Mary Anning said, "The dragon is gigantic!"

3. "Its eyes are as big as saucers!" she told her mother.

4. "I am inside the cave!" she shouted to her brother.

5. The scientists were amazed by the remarkable fossil.

B. Read each sentence. If the underlined verb is in the past tense, write *past* on the line. If it is in the present tense, write *present*.

1. Mary Anning <u>was</u> a real person. _____

2. I <u>am</u> interested in fossils, too. _____

3. There <u>are</u> many dinosaurs in the museum. _____

4. The exhibits <u>were</u> closed yesterday. _____

5. This <u>is</u> a map of the first floor. _____

C. Write the form of be that completes each sentence.

am   is   are

1. I _____ on the bus with my mother and father.

2. Buses _____ fun to ride.

3. The bus driver _____ a friendly woman.

Scholastic

*A **main verb** is the most important verb in a sentence. It shows the action. A*
***helping verb** works with the main verb. Forms of **be** and **have** are helping verbs.*

A. Read each sentence. Circle the helping verb. Draw a line under the main verb.

1. Jamal had built his first model rocket last year.

2. He has painted it red, white, and blue.

3. Now Jamal is building another rocket.

4. It will fly many feet into the air.

5. A parachute will bring the rocket back to Jamal.

6. I am buying a model rocket, too.

B. Complete each sentence with the correct main verb or helping verb in ( ). Write the word on the line.

1. Kim _____ making a clay vase. (is, has)

2. The clay _____ arrived yesterday. (was, had)

3. I am _____ to watch her work. (go, going)

4. She is _____ a potter's wheel. (used, using)

5. The sculpture _____ go above the fireplace. (will, is)

6. People _____ admired Kim's beautiful vases. (are, have)

C. Write two sentences about something you will do later in the week. Use the future tense helping verb. Be sure to use a main verb and helping verb in each sentence.

1. _____

2. _____

Scholastic

Irregular verbs *do not form the past tense by adding* **-ed**. *They change their form.*

A. In each sentence, underline the past tense of the verb in ( ). Then write the past-tense verb on the line.

1. Jessi told Jackie to be ready early. (tell) ———————————

2. He was nervous about his science fair project. (is) ———————————

3. Jackie's friends came to the table. (come) ———————————

4. They saw the volcano there. (see) ———————————

5. Jackie knew his speech by heart. (know) ———————————

6. The sign on the exhibit fell over. (fall) ———————————

7. The teacher lit the match for Jackie. (light) ———————————

8. Jackie threw his hands into the air. (throw) ———————————

B. Complete each sentence. Write the correct verb on the line.

fell   threw   saw   knew

1. Jackie ——————————— all about volcanoes.

2. He once ——————————— a real volcano.

3. It ——————————— ashes and fire into the air.

4. The ashes ——————————— all over the ground.

C. Complete each sentence. Use the past form of know in one and the past form of tell in the other.

1. When I was five, I ———————————

2. My brother ———————————

Scholastic

*An **adjective** is a word that describes a person, place, or thing.*

A. Read each sentence. Write the adjective on the line that describes the underlined noun.

1. We live near a sparkling <u>brook</u> _____

2. It has clear <u>water</u>. _____

3. Large <u>fish</u> swim in the brook. _____

4. Busy <u>squirrels</u> play near the brook. _____

5. You can enjoy breathing in the fresh <u>air</u> near the brook. _____

B. Complete each sentence by adding an adjective.

1. I love _____ apples.

2. I see a _____ ball.

3. I smell _____ flowers.

4. I hear _____ music.

5. I like the _____ taste of pickles.

Scholastic

The words a, an, *and* the *are special adjectives called* **articles**. **A** *is used before words that begin with a consonant.* **An** *is used before words that begin with a vowel.* **The** *is used before either.*

A. Circle the articles in each sentence.

1. The elk, moose, and bears grazed in the forest.

2. There was an abundant supply of grass and plants.

3. A bolt of lightning struck a tree and started a fire.

4. Fires have always been an important part of forest ecology.

5. The heat of the summer left the forest very dry.

6. The fires spread over a thousand acres.

7. The helicopters and an airplane spread chemicals on the fire.

8. Firefighters made an attempt to stop the flames.

B. Circle the article in ( ) that completes each sentence correctly. Then write it on the line.

1. Last summer I visited ———— National Park. (a, an)

2. We took a bus through ———— forests. (an, the)

3. The bus carried us up ———— narrow roads. (a, the)

4. I saw ———— elk grazing on some grass. (a, an)

5. We stayed in ———— old log cabin. (a, an)

6. Deer came up to ———— cabin window. (an, the)

7. We made ———— new friend. (a, an)

8. I wrote my friend ———— letter. (a, an)

Scholastic

*A **contraction** is a word that combines two smaller words. An apostrophe is added where letters have been left out. For example,* it is *becomes* it's.

A. Read and write each word. Then separate each contraction to write two smaller words.

List Words

1. where's   _____   _____   _____

2. wouldn't   _____   _____   _____

3. you'll   _____   _____   _____

4. haven't   _____   _____   _____

5. we've   _____   _____   _____

6. she's   _____   _____   _____

7. they'll   _____   _____   _____

8. shouldn't   _____   _____   _____

9. that's   _____   _____   _____

10. you've   _____   _____   _____

11. doesn't   _____   _____   _____

12. aren't   _____   _____   _____

Challenge Words

13. hour   _____

14. minute   _____

15. second   _____

B. Write four list words that are missing two letters in place of the apostrophe.

_____   _____   _____   _____

Scholastic

A. Circle a set of words that could be replaced with a contraction. Write the list word on the line.

1. We knew we would not be at the game. _____

2. Sydney said that she is going on vacation. _____

3. It does not look like a good day for the beach. _____

4. They will celebrate the team's victory. _____

5. Mom said that you have got to come inside. _____

6. I have not seen the new movie yet. _____

B. Circle each of the list words hidden in the puzzle. The words go across, down, backward, and diagonally. Write each word (including the apostrophe) in the correct group.

Across	Backward
_____	_____
_____	_____
_____	_____

Down	Diagonally
_____	_____
_____	_____
_____	_____

```
f  j  c  s  t  a  h  t  v  m  t
v  y  g  w  h  e  r  e  s  i  h
b  o  o  t  n  e  r  a  h  b  e
m  u  f  d  e  p  s  h  o  l  y
a  v  t  n  o  w  y  o  u  l  l
h  e  u  w  a  e  k  s  l  i  l
s  c  n  d  e  q  s  p  d  s  r
p  o  s  e  g  v  w  n  n  j  t
e  y  o  h  a  v  e  n  t  x  q
u  t  n  d  l  u  o  w  y  n  o
```

C. Write each challenge word followed by its definition.

7. _____

8. _____

9. _____

Scholastic

A **contraction** *is a word that combines two smaller words. An apostrophe is added where letters have been left out. For example,* it is *becomes* it's.

A. Underline the contraction in each sentence. Circle the apostrophe. Then write the contraction on the line.

1. It's time for another adventure. _____

2. We're studying animal habitats. _____

3. They've made a habitat for Bella. _____

4. I'm sure that Bella is gone. _____

5. Wanda thinks that she'll be back. _____

6. They're in favor of going to find Bella. _____

B. Circle the contraction. Then write the two words that make up the contraction.

1. I've gone on this bus before. _____

2. What's the bus doing? _____

3. It's shrinking to the size of a bullfrog. _____

4. The students say they're having fun. _____

5. "I'm hanging on for dear life," Liz said. _____

C. Put the two words together to form a contraction.

1. he + will = _____ **4.** I + am = _____

2. they + are = _____ **5.** we + will = _____

3. who + is = _____ **6.** there + is = _____

Scholastic

Quotation marks *show the exact words of a speaker.* **Commas** *appear between the day and year in a date, between the city and state in a location, and between the lines of an address.*

A. Add quotation marks to show the speaker's exact words.

1.   I have a strange case, said Mr. Brown.

2.   What's strange about it? asked Encyclopedia.

3.   Seventeen years ago Mr. Hunt found an elephant, began Mr. Brown.

4.   Where did he find it? asked Mrs. Brown.

5.   The elephant just appeared in his window, answered Mr. Brown.

6.   He must have fainted! exclaimed Encyclopedia.

7.   No, Mr. Hunt bought him, said Mr. Brown.

B.   Add commas wherever they are needed.

1.   I go to the library in Huntsville Alabama.

2.   It is located at 12 Oak Street Huntsville Alabama 36554.

3.   The last time I was there was January 8 2001.

4.   The books I checked out were due January 22 2001.

5.   My cousin Jeb goes to the branch library at 75 Peachtree Lane   Farley Alabama 35802.

6.   Is it true that Donald Sobol once spoke at the library in Redstone Park Alabama?

7.   He spoke there on September 29 2000.

8.   He will soon read at 47 Draper Road Newportville Pennsylvania.

Scholastic

*A **describing word** makes a sentence more interesting.*

Read the describing words found in the beach balls. Add the describing words to make each sentence more interesting. Write each new sentence.

1. The snow cone sat in the sun.

_____

2. Many children ran toward the ocean waves.

_____

3. My friends built a sandcastle.

_____

4. My brother grabbed his beach toys.

_____

5. Our dog tried to catch beach balls.

_____

Scholastic

Sometimes two sentences can be combined to make one sentence.

Sentences that share the same subject seem to go together like ketchup and mustard. Rewrite the sentences by combining their endings with the word *and*.

1. I ordered a hamburger.
I ordered a milkshake.

I ordered a hamburger and a milkshake.

2. I like salt on my French fries.
I like ketchup on my French fries.

_____

3. My mom makes great pork chops.
My mom makes great applesauce.

_____

4. My dad eats two huge helpings of meat loaf!
My dad eats two huge helpings of potatoes!

_____

5. My brother helps set the table.
My brother helps clean the dishes.

_____

6. We have cookies for dessert.
We have ice cream for dessert.

_____

Scholastic

A sentence includes a subject and a verb. A sentence is more interesting when it also includes a part that tells where, when, or why.

Add more information to each sentence by telling where, when, or why. Write the complete new sentence.

1. Mom is taking us shopping. Where?

_____

2. The stores are closing. When?

_____

3. We need to find a gift for Dad. Why?

_____

4. I will buy new jeans. Where?

_____

5. We may eat lunch. When?

_____

Scholastic

*A topic sentence is sometimes called the **main idea**.*

Read the groups of sentences. Then write a topic sentence that tells the main idea of the paragraph.

1.

_____

_____

One reason is that guinea pigs do not usually bite. Second, guinea pigs don't make as much noise as other rodents might during the night. Last, they are large enough that they can be found if they ever get lost in a house.

2.

_____

_____

First, spread peanut butter on two pieces of bread. Next, cut a banana into slices and lay them on top of the peanut butter. Then close the two pieces of bread into a sandwich. Last, eat up!

3.

_____

_____

Frogs usually have longer legs and wetter skin than toads do. Many frogs live near a water source of some kind while toads prefer a damp, muddy environment. Frog eggs and toad eggs are different in shape.

Scholastic

The sentence that tells the topic of a paragraph is called the **topic sentence**.

Draw a line through the sentence that does not belong with the topic.

1. Topic: Dogs make great family pets.

Dogs have great hearing, which helps them protect a family from danger.

Most dogs welcome their owners with wagging tails.

My favorite kind of dog is a boxer.

Many dogs are willing to play with children in a safe manner.

2. Topic: The history of the American flag is quite interesting.

The first American flag had 13 stars.

Not much is known about the history of Chinese flags.

Historians cannot prove that Betsy Ross really made the first American flag.

The American flag has changed 27 times.

3. Topic: Hurricanes are called by different names depending on where they occur.

Hurricanes have strong, powerful winds.

In the Philippines, hurricanes are called baguios.

Hurricanes are called typhoons in the Far East.

Australian people use the name willy-willies to describe hurricanes.

Scholastic

A good paragraph has at least three supporting sentences.

Finish the paragraphs below by writing three sentences that support each topic sentence.

Airplanes are useful in many ways. First, _____

_____

Second, _____

_____

Third, _____

_____

Life as a child today is quite different from the way it was when my

parents were young. First, _____

_____

Second, _____

_____

Third, _____

_____

Scholastic

Sentences can be written in order of beginning (B), middle (M), and ending (E) to make a paragraph.

Write a middle and ending sentence to complete each paragraph.

B **The circus started with a roll of drums and flashing lights.**

M Next, _____

E Last, _____

B **The tightrope walker stepped into the spotlight.**

M Next, _____

E Last, _____

B **The lion tamer came on stage.**

M Next, _____

E Last, _____

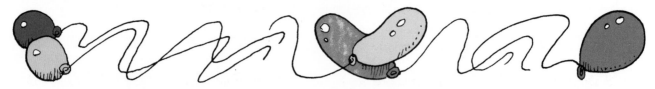

B **The dancing ponies appeared in the center ring.**

M Next, _____

E Last, _____

Scholastic

*The **closing sentence** retells the topic sentence or main idea of a paragraph.*

Write a closing sentence for each paragraph.

All cyclists should wear helmets while riding their bikes. Many injuries occur to the head in biking accidents. Helmets could help prevent the injuries. Helmets also make cyclists more easily noticed by car drivers. _____

_____

There are many things to do on a rainy day. If you like to write, you could send a letter to a friend or make a book. If you prefer craft projects, you could make a bookmark or a collage. If you really enjoy games, you could play cards or build a puzzle. _____

_____

The wheel must be one of the world's most important inventions. First, we would have no means of transportation if it were not for wheels. Second, we would not be able to enjoy many of our favorite pastimes, like in-line skating and riding a bike. Last, it would be very difficult to move heavy objects around without wheels. _____

_____

Scholastic

Use a paragraph plan before you begin writing.

It is time to plan and write your own paragraph. You may want to use your own topic or one of the following topics: My Favorite Vacation, Collecting Coins, Our Pet Snake.

1. **Choose a topic.** _____

2. **Brainstorm three supporting ideas.**

    a) _____

    b) _____

    c) _____

3. **Write a topic sentence.** _____

4. **Write a closing sentence.** _____

Use the plan to write your own paragraph.

_____

_____

_____

_____

_____

_____

_____

_____

Scholastic

*A **persuasive paragraph** gives your opinion and tries to convince the reader to agree. Its supporting ideas are reasons that back up your opinion.*

Reason 1

Topic sentence

→ Our family should have a dog for three reasons.

First, pets teach responsibility. If we get a dog, I will

feed him and take him for walks after school. The

second reason for having a pet is that he would ← *Reason 2*

make a good companion for me when everyone else is busy. I

Reason 3

won't drive Dad crazy always asking him to play catch with me. The ←

third reason we need a dog is for safety. He would warn us of

danger and keep our house safe. For all of these reasons, I'm sure

you'll agree that we should jump in the car and head toward the

adoption agency right away. I don't know how we have made it ← *Closing sentence*

this long without a dog!

Plan and write a persuasive paragraph asking your parents for something (such as a family trip, expensive new shoes, or an in-ground pool).

1. Choose a topic._____

2. Write a topic sentence. _____

3. Brainstorm three supporting reasons.

Reason 1 _____

Reason 2 _____

Reason 3 _____

4. Write a closing sentence: _____

Scholastic

An **expository paragraph** *provides facts or explains ideas. The supporting sentences give more details about the topic.*

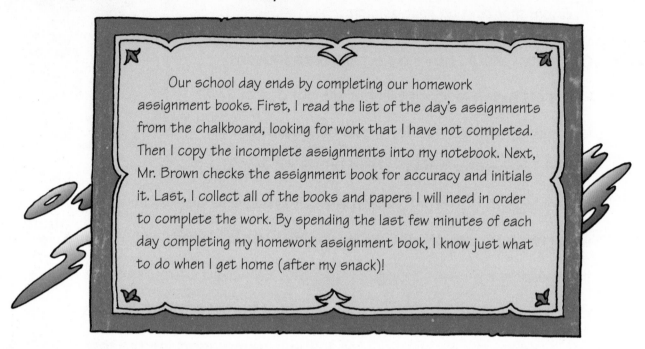

Our school day ends by completing our homework assignment books. First, I read the list of the day's assignments from the chalkboard, looking for work that I have not completed. Then I copy the incomplete assignments into my notebook. Next, Mr. Brown checks the assignment book for accuracy and initials it. Last, I collect all of the books and papers I will need in order to complete the work. By spending the last few minutes of each day completing my homework assignment book, I know just what to do when I get home (after my snack)!

Plan and write an expository paragraph explaining one part of your school day.

Write the topic sentence. _____

_____

List the four supporting ideas.

1) _____

2) _____

3) _____

4) _____

Write the closing sentence. _____

_____

Scholastic

*The five parts of a **personal letter** include the date, greeting, body, closing, and signature. Notice the punctuation marks that are used in each part.*

August 13, 2003 ◄— *date*

greeting —► Dear Gramps,

body —► We had a great fishing trip! Dad caught two bass. I hooked an enormous catfish, but he got away. I guess Swan Lake is lucky for us. I'll always remember this trip.

Love, ◄— *closing*

John ◄— *signature*

Write a letter to an out-of-town family member. For the body of your letter, write an expository paragraph using the plan on page 178.

_____
(today's date)

_____ ,

_____

_____

_____

_____

_____

_____

_____ ,

_____
(your name)

Grammar/Writing Practice Test

Fill in the bubble next to the correct answer.

1. Which is a complete sentence?

    ◯ **A**   Friendly parents

    ◯ **B**   My parents are

    ◯ **C**   Very famous

    ◯ **D**   My parents are friendly and generous.

2. Which type of sentence is the following?
    Look at that horse.

    ◯ **F**   telling

    ◯ **G**   question

    ◯ **H**   exclamation

    ◯ **J**   command

3. Which noun is a proper noun?

    ◯ **A**   Yellowstone National Park

    ◯ **B**   zoo

    ◯ **C**   planetarium

    ◯ **D**   museum

Scholastic

Grammar/Writing Practice Test

Fill in the bubble next to the correct answer.

4. Which sentence is correct?

○ **A** our teacher is dr. Ruffin

○ **B** Our teacher, Dr. ruffin, is from louisiana.

○ **C** Our teacher, Dr. Ruffin, is from louisiana

○ **D** Our teacher, Dr. Ruffin, is from Louisiana.

5. Which word is the action verb in the following sentence?
The villagers happily cheered loudly.

○ **F** the

○ **G** happily

○ **H** cheered

○ **J** loudly

6. Which pronoun would take the place of "my friends" in the following sentence?
My friends read a story aloud to the children in the hospital.

○ **A** it

○ **B** us

○ **C** she

○ **D** they

Scholastic

Grammar/Writing Practice Test

Fill in the bubble next to the correct answer.

7. Which word is the linking verb in the following sentence?
They are hard workers and wonderful friends.

- ○ **A**   they
- ○ **B**   are
- ○ **C**   and
- ○ **D**   workers

8. Which word is the simple predicate in the following sentence?
All the children looked at the purple cow with amazement.

- ○ **F**   looked
- ○ **G**   all
- ○ **H**   amazement
- ○ **J**   children

9. Which word in the simple subject in the following sentence?
Many people visited the museum that day.

- ○ **A**   many
- ○ **B**   people
- ○ **C**   visited
- ○ **D**   museum

Scholastic

Grammar/Writing Practice Test

Choose a sticker to place here.

Fill in the bubble next to the correct answer.

10. Read the sentence. Identify the error.

The kids at Elm School had been waiting for a snowstorm?

- ○ **A**   kids
- ○ **B**   had been
- ○ **C**   question mark
- ○ **D**   correct as is

11. Read the sentence. Identify the error.

they knew school would be canceled if the storm brought a lot of snow.

- ○ **F**   they
- ○ **G**   school
- ○ **H**   canceled
- ○ **J**   period

12. Read the sentence. Identify the error.

It snowed twelve inches, so School was canceled.

- ○ **A**   snowed
- ○ **B**   School
- ○ **C**   twelve
- ○ **D**   period

Scholastic

Addition & Subtraction

Understanding basic addition and subtraction facts is an important real-life skill. When you buy things you need to know how to add up the cost of the items and how to figure out the change you will receive after you have paid for them. We probably add and/or subtract things several times every day.

What to Do

These activity pages provide many opportunities for your child to practice addition and subtraction with and without regrouping. Remember, when you regroup, you carry over from the right-hand column to the left-hand column. For example:

$$
\begin{array}{r}
\overset{1}{2}19 \\
+\ \ 5 \\
\hline
224
\end{array}
$$

Some of the subtraction problems will require that your child borrow from the number to the left. For example:

$$
\begin{array}{r}
1\overset{0}{\cancel{1}}\overset{1}{5} \\
-\ \ \ 7 \\
\hline
1\ 0\ 8
\end{array}
$$

Check your child's work when he or she finishes each activity page. For your convenience, you will find the answers at the back of the workbook.

Keep On Going!

Encourage your child to become an addition and subtraction "pro." Create addition and subtraction problems based on your child's activities for the day. For example: If you need $15 to go to the movies and you only have $3, how much money will you need to earn to be able to buy a ticket? Or, you have a 3-page paper due on Monday. You have already written 2 pages. How many more pages will you need to write to finish the paper?

Add.

1. + 3 | 15 | 18 | 4 | 7 | 12 | 15

2. + 5 | 13 | 11 | 9

3. + 7 | 11 | 8 | 10

4. + 2 | 6 | 16 | 13

5. + 6 | 12 | 3 | 9

6. + 8 | 4 | 1 | 10

7. + 9 | 7 | 2 | 8

8. + 4 | 9 | 7 | 14

9. + 10 | 4 | 8 | 6

...in

10. + 1 | 3 | 8 | 1

1492!

 In 1492, Columbus sailed to America with these ships: the *Pinta*, the *Nina*, and the *Santa Maria*. Add the number of these ships to the number of ships in the picture.

Scholastic

Subtract. Then use the code to write a letter for each difference to see what the Pilgrims packed for Plymouth. Put an **X** on the item the Pilgrims did not pack.

1.

15 − 1	16 − 8	15 − 13	13 − 8	16 − 5

○ ○ ○ ○ ○

2.

7 − 5	15 − 8	17 − 6

○ ○ ○

3.

18 − 14	11 − 9	17 − 12	16 − 15	17 − 0

○ ○ ○ ○ ○

4.

18 − 4	10 − 8	18 − 8	12 − 1	15 − 11

○ ○ ○ ○ ○

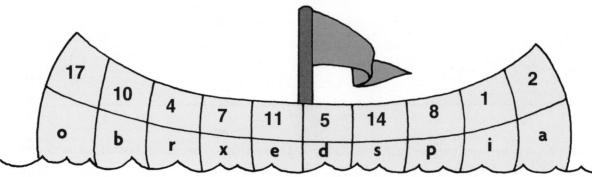

17	10	4	7	11	5	14	8	1	2
o	b	r	x	e	d	s	p	i	a

Scholastic

Add or subtract. Connect the matching answers
to find each state's shape.

1.	Delaware	**16 – 9 =**
2.	Massachusetts	**7 + 7 =**
3.	New Hampshire	**15 – 6 =**
4.	New York	**17 + 1 =**
5.	South Carolina	**14 – 3 =**
6.	Maryland	**15 – 2 =**
7.	Pennsylvania	**14 – 9 =**
8.	Connecticut	**12 + 5 =**
9.	Rhode Island	**7 + 3 =**
10.	North Carolina	**13 – 7 =**
11.	Georgia	**7 + 5 =**
12.	New Jersey	**14 – 6 =**
13.	Virginia	**7 + 8 =**

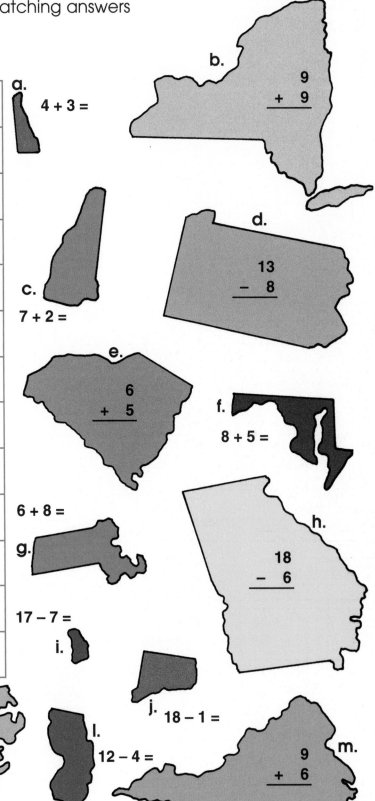

a. **4 + 3 =**

b.
9
+ 9

c. **7 + 2 =**

d.
13
– 8

e.
6
+ 5

f. **8 + 5 =**

g. **6 + 8 =**

h.
18
– 6

i. **17 – 7 =**

j. **18 – 1 =**

k.
15
– 9

l. **12 – 4 =**

m.
9
+ 6

Scholastic

Add. Use the code to write words that tell about
our past.

1.

63	12	65	62	34	24	41	53
+ 12	+ 11	+ 33	+ 24	+ 13	+ 10	+ 34	+ 46

◯ ◯ ◯ ◯ ◯ ◯ ◯ ◯

2.

40	26	23	35	21	53	22	13	64	68
+ 46	+ 72	+ 10	+ 43	+ 43	+ 34	+ 10	+ 34	+ 14	+ 31

◯ ◯ ◯ ◯ ◯ ◯ ◯ ◯ ◯ ◯

3.

31	25	21	44	76	21	11
+ 33	+ 22	+ 30	+ 54	+ 10	+ 11	+ 10

◯ ◯ ◯ ◯ ◯ ◯ ◯

4.

40	35	44	52
+ 11	+ 63	+ 20	+ 12

◯ ◯ ◯ ◯

Code

21 Y	23 M	32 T	33 V	34 C	42 P	47 I	51 B
64 L	69 D	75 A	78 O	86 R	87 U	98 E	99 N

Scholastic

Add. Write the letters in the circles to identify each president.

1.   **I was a leader in the Civil War.**

39 + 13	38 + 15	56 + 26	26 + 35	29 + 67	27 + 25	43 + 39

◯ ◯ ◯ ◯ ◯ ◯ ◯

2.   **I helped write the Declaration of Independence.**

19 + 18	28 + 55	24 + 18	19 + 23	17 + 66	59 + 19	49 + 15	78 + 18	48 + 34

◯ ◯ ◯ ◯ ◯ ◯ ◯ ◯ ◯

3.   **I was a leader in the American Revolutionary War.**

59 + 39	48 + 24	27 + 37	19 + 46	27 + 26	38 + 44	27 + 18	18 + 29	38 + 58	27 + 55

◯ ◯ ◯ ◯ ◯ ◯ ◯ ◯ ◯ ◯

Code

61 C	98 W	55 Y	83 E	45 G	82 N	78 R	65 H	52 L
96 O	42 F	86 K	47 T	72 A	37 J	64 S	53 I	36 D

Scholastic

Subtract. Draw a line from each difference to the vacation spot on the map.

1.

Mount Rushmore	Niagara Falls	Gateway Arch	Four Corners Monument	Statue of Liberty
72 − 27	57 − 29	58 − 39	93 − 19	94 − 29

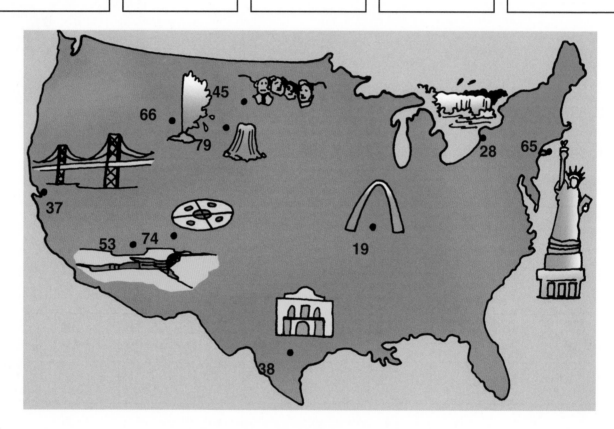

2.

Grand Canyon	Devil's Tower	Golden Gate Bridge	The Alamo	Old Faithful
82 − 29	93 − 14	64 − 27	66 − 28	94 − 28

Scholastic

Add or subtract. Use the chart to color the picture.

white	blue	brown	red	yellow
0–20	21–40	41–60	61–80	81–100

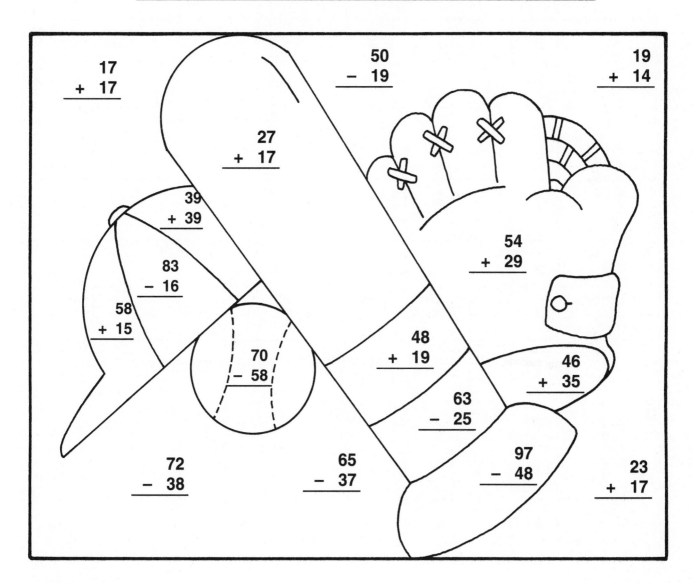

17
+ 17

50
− 19

19
+ 14

27
+ 17

39
+ 39

83
− 16

58
+ 15

54
+ 29

70
− 58

48
+ 19

46
+ 35

63
− 25

72
− 38

65
− 37

97
− 48

23
+ 17

Finish the pattern.

32   34   36   ____   ____   42   ____   46   ____   ____

Scholastic

Add. Fill in the missing numbers.

1.
```
    3  2  4
+   6  3  □
─────────────
   □  □  6
```

2.
```
    2  4  □
+   □  5  1
─────────────
    7  □  2
```

3.
```
   □  5  5
+  3  □  1
─────────────
   4  8  □
```

4.
```
    2  □  3
+   □  1  3
─────────────
    5  2  □
```

5.
```
    4  1  □
+   3  □  2
─────────────
   □  3  7
```

6.
```
   □  4  3
+  1  4  □
─────────────
   2  □  9
```

7.
```
    2  □  □
+   2  1  6
─────────────
   □  1  8
```

8.
```
   □  3  1
+  4  □  □
─────────────
   8  5  3
```

9.
```
    1  □  2
+   □  3  3
─────────────
    3  7  □
```

10.
```
   □  4  1
+  1  3  □
─────────────
   6  □  5
```

11.
```
    3  3  □
+   □  □  3
─────────────
    6  6  8
```

12.
```
   □  1  2
+  2  □  2
─────────────
   9  4  □
```

13.
```
    2  2  □
+   3  1  4
─────────────
   □  □  4
```

14.
```
    5  □  4
+   □  3  4
─────────────
    8  4  □
```

15.
```
    2  2  4
+   1  □  3
─────────────
   □  6  □
```

16.
```
   □  1  6
+  1  3  □
─────────────
   5  □  8
```

 Joe and Ellie were going to the movies. Joe brought $5.□0, and Ellie brought $□.35. If they had $9.75 altogether, how much money did they each have? Show your work.

Scholastic

Add.

P X O V Q Z
W N O U T R Y S

1.	298 + 276	191 + 343	269 + 289
2.	157 + 189	137 + 369	278 + 485
3.	395 + 457	244 + 279	499 + 446
4.	288 + 664	236 + 288	577 + 388
5.	498 + 399	399 + 164	284 + 439

6.	259 + 467	364 + 258	487 + 436
7.	199 + 128	199 + 89	238 + 287
8.	255 + 373	509 + 315	117 + 304
9.	257 + 569	276 + 566	149 + 279
10.	339 + 385	258 + 467	179 + 348

This letter names an icy drink.

Color each answer with a 5 in the hundreds place to see!

This letter names an insect that stings.

Color each answer with a 2 in the tens place to see!

Scholastic

Add or subtract. Match each person to the correct mailbox sum.

1. My mailbox has a 4, 9, and 3. The 9 is in the ones place.

2. My mailbox has a 7, 6, and 2. The 2 is in the hundreds place.

3. My mailbox has a 1, 5, and 5. The 1 is in the ones place.

4. My mailbox has a 4, 9, and 3. The 9 is in the hundreds place.

5. My mailbox has a 2, 7, and 6. The 2 is in the ones place.

6. My mailbox has a 5, 1, and 5. The 1 is in the hundreds place.

7. My mailbox has a 4, 9, and 3. The 9 is in the tens place.

8. My mailbox has a 5, 5, and 1. The 1 is in the tens place.

9. My mailbox has a 2, 7, and 6. The 2 is in the tens place.

a.
$$287 + 206$$
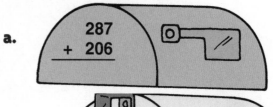

b.
$$188 + 88$$
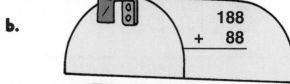

c.
$$914 - 287$$
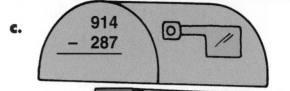

d.
$$835 - 486$$
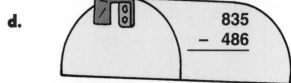

e.
$$99 + 56$$
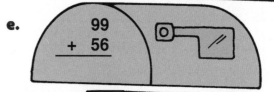

f.
$$466 + 468$$
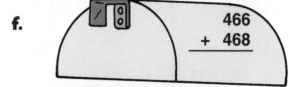

g.
$$950 - 188$$
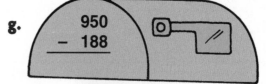

h.
$$152 + 363$$
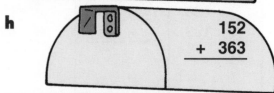

i.
$$273 + 278$$
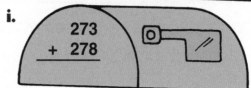

Scholastic

Use the coordinates to find each number. Add or subtract.

A	496	723	379
B	162	215	956
C	547	834	688
	1	2	3

E	668	884	345
F	239	716	188
G	422	578	957
	4	5	6

A. (A, 1)
(F, 6) − ____

B. (B, 3)
(E, 4) − ____

C. (C, 1)
(F, 4) + ____

D. (A, 3)
(E, 6) + ____

E. (A, 2)
(B, 1) − ____

F. (G, 4)
(B, 2) − ____

G. (G, 6)
(C, 3) − ____

H. (E, 5)
(C, 2) + ____

I. (B, 3)
(G, 5) − ____

Color the largest number on each house orange. Color the smallest number on each house purple.

Scholastic

Add or subtract.

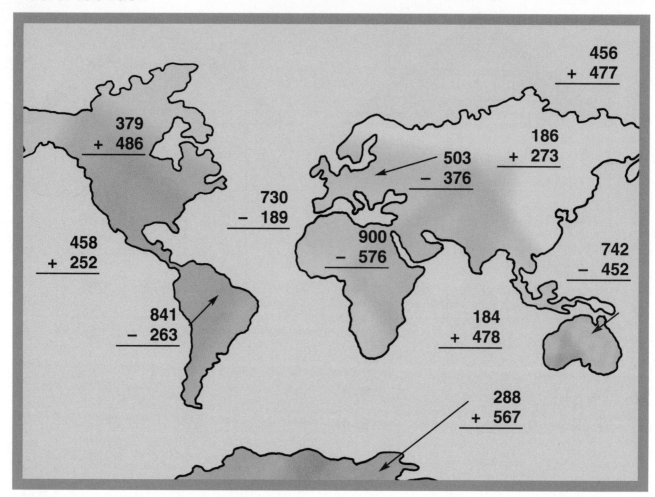

Label the map using the code below.

North America	> 860 and < 927	**Atlantic Ocean**	> 496 and < 560
South America	> 571 and < 658	**Indian Ocean**	> 581 and < 672
Australia	> 189 and < 293	**Pacific Ocean**	> 671 and < 732
Asia	> 423 and < 538	**Arctic Ocean**	> 867 and < 948
Europe	> 85 and < 266		
Antarctica	> 748 and < 864		
Africa	> 297 and < 334		

  Add the answers for the oceans together.

Scholastic

Add or subtract. Use the code to name four
different mountain ranges.

N	6,348
R	8,789
A	5,063
I	7,695
O	2,429
K	5,642
E	7,483
C	3,012
Y	2,351
Z	5,234
L	3,721
U	6,704
P	3,827
S	8,749
D	4,907

1.
2,033
+ 3,030

2.
2,411
+ 1,310

3.
2,504
+ 1,323

4.
4,328
+ 4,421

5.
4,258
+ 4,531

6.
1,326
+ 1,103

7.
1,012
+ 2,000

8.
2,321
+ 3,321

9.
1,231
+ 1,120

10.
1,204
+ 1,225

11.
2,113
+ 3,121

12.
2,042
+ 3,021

13.
3,746
+ 5,043

14.
4,131
+ 1,511

15.
4,053
+ 1,010

16.
2,216
+ 4,132

17.
2,506
+ 2,401

18.
6,471
+ 1,012

19.
7,326
+ 1,423

Scholastic

Add. Match the sums to show the hats and shoes that go together.

1.
$$2,976 \\ + 5,787$$

2.
$$3,575 \\ + 2,477$$

3.
$$2,547 \\ + 2,787$$

4.
$$2,459 \\ + 1,558$$

5.
$$6,538 \\ + 2,862$$

6.
$$3,798 \\ + 3,559$$

7.
$$1,586 \\ + 1,866$$

a.
$$2,386 \\ + 3,666$$

b.
$$1,278 \\ + 2,739$$

c.
$$2,645 \\ + 4,712$$

d.
$$3,885 \\ + 4,878$$

e.
$$1,665 \\ + 1,787$$

f.
$$3,655 \\ + 1,679$$

g.
$$2,766 \\ + 6,634$$

Scholastic

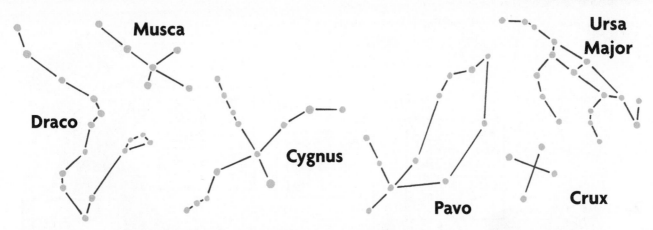

Musca
Draco
Cygnus
Ursa Major
Pavo
Crux

Subtract. Draw a line between matching sums to connect the Latin and English names for each constellation.

Latin

1.
Draco
$$\begin{array}{r} 7,621 \\ -\ 5,586 \\ \hline \end{array}$$

2.
Pavo
$$\begin{array}{r} 7,340 \\ -\ 3,758 \\ \hline \end{array}$$

3.
Cygnus
$$\begin{array}{r} 9,317 \\ -\ 2,858 \\ \hline \end{array}$$

4.
Ursa Major
$$\begin{array}{r} 8,332 \\ -\ 3,579 \\ \hline \end{array}$$

5.
Musca
$$\begin{array}{r} 7,015 \\ -\ 1,739 \\ \hline \end{array}$$

6.
Crux
$$\begin{array}{r} 8,150 \\ -\ 3,166 \\ \hline \end{array}$$

English

a.
$$\begin{array}{r} 8,533 \\ -\ 2,074 \\ \hline \end{array}$$
Swan

b.
$$\begin{array}{r} 7,662 \\ -\ 2,678 \\ \hline \end{array}$$
Cross

c.
$$\begin{array}{r} 8,403 \\ -\ 6,368 \\ \hline \end{array}$$
Dragon

d.
$$\begin{array}{r} 6,441 \\ -\ 2,859 \\ \hline \end{array}$$
Peacock

e.
$$\begin{array}{r} 7,031 \\ -\ 2,278 \\ \hline \end{array}$$
Great Bear

f.
$$\begin{array}{r} 8,133 \\ -\ 2,857 \\ \hline \end{array}$$
Fly

Scholastic

Add or subtract. Then write the problem's letter
above its matching answer below.

1. W.
$$2,376 + 2,784$$

2. O.
$$8,500 - 2,763$$

3. T.
$$4,401 - 2,550$$

7. A.
$$2,763 + 3,857$$

4. E.
$$6,345 - 2,660$$

5. H.
$$8,455 - 1,867$$

6. !
$$4,672 + 3,885$$

11. M.
$$8,304 - 2,541$$

9. M.
$$2,463 + 4,908$$

8. A.
$$1,074 + 5,988$$

10. E.
$$4,365 - 1,478$$

12. S.
$$3,453 + 2,778$$

___ ___ ___ ___ is
5,763 7,062 1,851 6,588

___ ___ ___ ___ ___ ___ ___ ___
6,620 5,160 2,887 6,231 5,737 7,371 3,685 8,557

Scholastic

Solve the problems below by making easy numbers. Look for numbers that add to 10, 20, 30, or other easy tens numbers. See the examples here.

Examples:

20 + 4 = 24	20 + 30 = 50	6 + 8 + 4 = 6 + 4 + 8 = 10 + 8 = 18	5 + 4 + 10 + 6 = 4 + 6 + 5 + 10 = 10 + 5 + 10 = 10 + 10 + 5 = 25

1. 7 + 3 + 5 = _____

2. 5 + 9 + 5 = _____

3. 4 + 4 + 6 = _____

4. 9 + 8 + 1 = _____

5. 2 + 7 + 8 = _____

6. 7 + 18 + 2 = _____

7. 29 + 10 + 1 = _____

8. 17 + 6 + 3 = _____

9. 25 + 8 + 5 = _____

10. 36 + 4 + 7 = _____

11. 52 + 7 + 1 + 8 = _____

12. 75 + 3 + 5 = _____

Write About It

What do you look for when making easy numbers?

_____

_____

Scholastic

Solve the problems below by making easy numbers.
Look for numbers that add to 10, 20, 30, or other easy
tens numbers. Before you start, look at the examples.

Examples of easy numbers:

60 + 7 = 67	6 + 28 + 4 = 6 + 4 + 28 = 10 + 28 = 38	7 + 16 + 3 + 20 = 10 + 16 + 20 = 26 + 20 = 46

1. 8 + 12 + 2 = _____

2. 8 + 17 + 2 = _____

3. 23 + 14 + 6 = _____

4. 14 + 25 + 6 = _____

5. 32 + 8 + 40 = _____

6. 87 + 6 + 4 = _____

7. 25 + 25 + 12 = _____

8. 95 + 14 + 5 = _____

9. 9 + 110 + 21 = _____

10. 22 + 8 + 160 = _____

11. 37 + 14 + 3 + 6 = _____

12. 5 + 23 + 55 + 10 = _____

13. 6 + 122 + 8 + 4 = _____

14. 340 + 3 + 7 + 12 = _____

15. 13 + 418 + 7 + 4 = _____

Write About It

How did you solve problem 12?

_____

_____

Scholastic

Addition & Subtraction Practice Test

Fill in the bubble next to the correct answer.

1.
$$488$$
$$+ 487$$

- ○ **A** 600
- ○ **B** 975
- ○ **C** 995
- ○ **D** 8

2.
$$3787$$
$$+ 4276$$

- ○ **F** 8163
- ○ **G** 8216
- ○ **H** 7063
- ○ **J** 8063

3.
$$2585$$
$$+ 3756$$

- ○ **A** 5341
- ○ **B** 6341
- ○ **C** 7341
- ○ **D** 6214

4.
$$4999$$
$$+ 3899$$

- ○ **F** 8698
- ○ **G** 8989
- ○ **H** 8898
- ○ **J** 7898

Scholastic

Addition & Subtraction Practice Test

Fill in the bubble next to the correct answer.

5.
$$
\begin{array}{r}
740 \\
- 357 \\
\hline
\end{array}
$$

- A   21
- B   383
- C   24
- D   25

7.
$$
\begin{array}{r}
5787 \\
- 2976 \\
\hline
\end{array}
$$

- A   3811
- B   2811
- C   2281
- D   3711

6.
$$
\begin{array}{r}
823 \\
- 649 \\
\hline
\end{array}
$$

- F   172
- G   274
- H   174
- J   162

8.
$$
\begin{array}{r}
3655 \\
- 1679 \\
\hline
\end{array}
$$

- F   2976
- G   2767
- H   1766
- J   1976

Scholastic

Addition & Subtraction Practice Test

Fill in the bubble next to the correct answer.

9.   15 + _____ = 125

- ○ **A**   100
- ○ **B**   110
- ○ **C**   120
- ○ **D**   155

11.   _____ – 53 = 126

- ○ **A**   179
- ○ **B**   159
- ○ **C**   163
- ○ **D**   150

10.   _____ + 236 = 286

- ○ **F**   45
- ○ **G**   55
- ○ **H**   50
- ○ **J**   40

12.   289 – 63 = _____

- ○ **F**   236
- ○ **G**   226
- ○ **H**   225
- ○ **J**   235

Scholastic

Multiplication & Division

When you multiply, you add a number to itself a number of times. For example: $4 + 4 + 4 + 4 + 4 = 20$ or $4 \times 5 = 20$. Multiplying is a quick way to add things up.

When you divide, you group numbers into equal parts. In the example $10 \div 2 = 5$, you group 10 into 2 equal parts of 5. To check your answer, you do the opposite of division—you multiply $5 \times 2 = 10$.

Sometimes you can't group all the numbers into equal parts. In those cases you will have a remainder, a number left over. For example: $38 \div 6 = 6$, remainder 2.

What to Do

Have your child solve the multiplication and division problems on the activity pages. Review the answers with your child. Remind your child that he or she can check the division problems by multiplying. In the example $38 \div 6 = 6$ remainder 2, multiply $6 \times 6 + 2 = 38$. Your answer is correct! An answer key is provided at the back of the book for your convenience.

On some of the activity pages your child is asked to color the page according to the answers to the problems. That will uncover a beautiful picture or quilt design.

Keep On Going!

Show your child that math can be fun by playing a multiplication/division game together. Give your child a multiplication problem and have him or her solve it and then turn it into a division problem to check the answer. For example:

$$7 \times 4 = 28$$
$$28 \div 4 = 7$$
or
$$28 \div 7 = 4$$

A **number line** can be used to help you multiply. One factor tells you how long each jump should be. This is like skip-counting. The other factor tells you how many jumps to take.

$2 \times 6 = 12$

x 2 | 0 2 4 6 8 10 12 14 16 18 20 22 24 26 28 30

$3 \times 3 = 9$

x 3 | 0 3 6 9 12 15 18 21 24 27 30

Use the number lines above to help you multiply by 2s and 3s.

A. $2 \times 2 =$ _____ $3 \times 3 =$ _____ $6 \times 2 =$ _____

B. $4 \times 3 =$ _____ $9 \times 2 =$ _____ $7 \times 3 =$ _____

C. $7 \times 2 =$ _____ $6 \times 3 =$ _____ $5 \times 2 =$ _____

 When multiplying by 0, the product is always 0. When multiplying by 1, the product is always the other factor.

D.

1	8	2	0	3	2
x 2	x 3	x 5	x 3	x 2	x 7

E.

4	3	1	6	0	3
x 2	x 3	x 3	x 2	x 2	x 1

Scholastic

Multiply. Then write the letter of the problem that matches each product below to learn the names of two of the brightest stars.

1. B. 3 x 4

2. R. 1 x 4

3. A. 2 x 4

4. F. 8 x 4

5. P. 7 x 4

6. S. 6 x 5

7. U. 3 x 5

8. E. 1 x 5

9. U. 4 x 4

10. I. 5 x 5

11. G. 0 x 5

12. S. 2 x 5

13. O. 4 x 5 = _____

14. D. 9 x 5 = _____

15. I. 9 x 4 = _____

16. N. 6 x 4 = _____

16. S. 7 x 5 = _____

17. C. 5 x 8 = _____

Two of the brightest stars are

___ ___ ___ ___ ___ ___ **and** ___ ___ ___ ___ ___ ___ ___ .
10 25 4 36 16 30   40 8 24 20 28 15 35

Scholastic

Multiply each number in the center by the numbers on the tire. Write your answers inside the wheel.

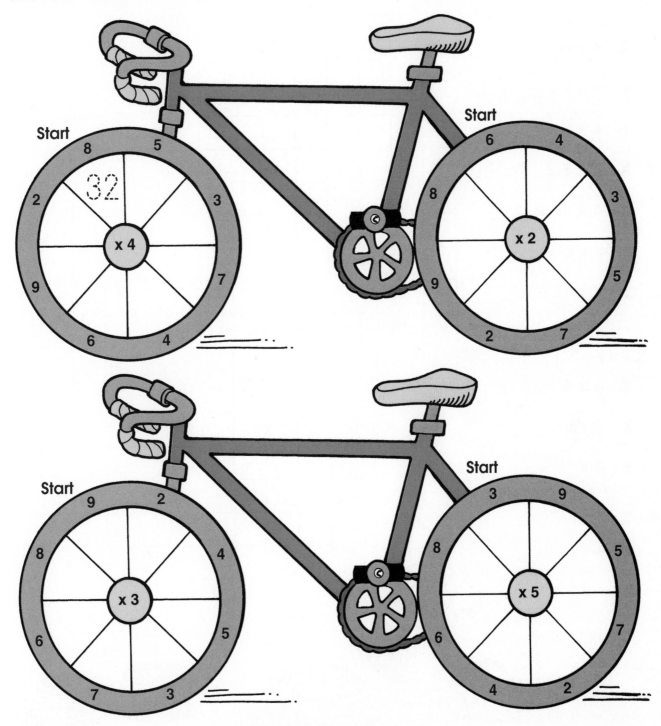

 The bike team has 4 members. Each biker rides 9 miles every day. How many miles does the team ride every day altogether?

Scholastic

Multiply. Write the number word for each product in the puzzle. Don't forget the hyphens!

Across

2. 4 x 9 = _____

4. 4 x 5 = _____

7. 4 x 3 = _____

8. 4 x 7 = _____

9. 4 x 10 = _____

11. 4 x 0 = _____

12. 4 x 11 = _____

Down

1. 4 x 4 = _____

2. 4 x 8 = _____

3. 4 x 12 = _____

5. 4 x 2 = _____

6. 4 x 6 = _____

10. 4 x 1 = _____

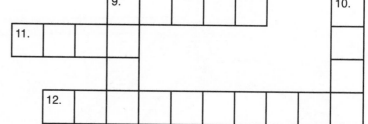

Tracy was missing 4 buttons on 11 different shirts. How many buttons does she need to fix all the shirts?

Complete each multiplication sentence. Then circle each answer in the picture.

A. 2 x 5 = _____

B. 5 x _____ = 5

C. _____ x 5 = 35

D. 10 x 5 = _____

E. _____ x 5 = 60

F. 5 x 6 = _____

G. _____ x 5 = 55

H. 5 x 3 = _____

I. 8 x 5 = _____

J. _____ x 5 = 45

K. 2 x _____ = 10

L. _____ x 5 = 25

M. 7 x 5 = _____

N. 5 x 12 = _____

O. 5 x _____ = 20

 Squeaky Squirrel lived in a tree with 4 squirrel friends. If each squirrel collected 12 nuts, how many nuts altogether did the squirrels collect?

Scholastic

Multiply.

$$5 \times 2 = \underline{\hspace{2em}}$$

$$\begin{array}{r} 4 \\ \times\ 6 \\ \hline \end{array}$$

$$\begin{array}{r} 2 \\ \times\ 6 \\ \hline \end{array}$$

$$\begin{array}{r} 3 \\ \times\ 7 \\ \hline \end{array}$$

$$\begin{array}{r} 7 \\ \times\ 3 \\ \hline \end{array}$$

$$\begin{array}{r} 7 \\ \times\ 1 \\ \hline \end{array}$$

$$6 \times 8 = \underline{\hspace{2em}}$$

$$\begin{array}{r} 3 \\ \times\ 6 \\ \hline \end{array}$$

$$\begin{array}{r} 5 \\ \times\ 6 \\ \hline \end{array}$$

$$\begin{array}{r} 6 \\ \times\ 5 \\ \hline \end{array}$$

$$\begin{array}{r} 4 \\ \times\ 7 \\ \hline \end{array}$$

$$7 \times 5 = \underline{\hspace{2em}}$$

$$\begin{array}{r} 3 \\ \times\ 7 \\ \hline \end{array}$$

$$6 \times 6 = \underline{\hspace{2em}}$$

$$\begin{array}{r} 9 \\ \times\ 7 \\ \hline \end{array}$$

$$\begin{array}{r} 6 \\ \times\ 7 \\ \hline \end{array}$$

$$\begin{array}{r} 6 \\ \times\ 4 \\ \hline \end{array}$$

$$\begin{array}{r} 3 \\ \times\ 7 \\ \hline \end{array}$$

$$\begin{array}{r} 7 \\ \times\ 9 \\ \hline \end{array}$$

$$\begin{array}{r} 7 \\ \times\ 7 \\ \hline \end{array}$$

$$9 \times 6 = \underline{\hspace{2em}}$$

$$\begin{array}{r} 8 \\ \times\ 6 \\ \hline \end{array}$$

$$\begin{array}{r} 7 \\ \times\ 6 \\ \hline \end{array}$$

$$8 \times 7 = \underline{\hspace{2em}}$$

$$5 \times 6 = \underline{\hspace{2em}}$$

$$7 \times 4 = \underline{\hspace{2em}}$$

 Color by using the following product code.

0–10 = purple	21–30 = blue	41–50 = yellow	61–70 = pink
11–20 = orange	31–40 = red	51–60 = green	

Scholastic

Multiply to get the lion back to its little cub.

$9 \times 8 =$ _____

$\begin{array}{r} 9 \\ \times\ 2 \\ \hline \end{array}$

$8 \times 5 =$ _____

$9 \times 4 =$ _____

$3 \times 8 =$ _____

$\begin{array}{r} 6 \\ \times\ 8 \\ \hline \end{array}$

$8 \times 1 =$ _____

$9 \times 9 =$ _____

$8 \times 4 =$ _____

$\begin{array}{r} 8 \\ \times\ 7 \\ \hline \end{array}$

$6 \times 9 =$ _____

$8 \times 8 =$ _____

$9 \times 3 =$ _____

$\begin{array}{r} 8 \\ \times\ 2 \\ \hline \end{array}$

$9 \times 0 =$ _____

$5 \times 9 =$ _____

There are 8 lions in the jungle. Each has 2 cubs. How many cubs are there altogether?

Scholastic

Multiply.

A. $\begin{array}{r} 9 \\ \times\ 6 \\ \hline \end{array}$ $\begin{array}{r} 8 \\ \times\ 9 \\ \hline \end{array}$ $\begin{array}{r} 8 \\ \times\ 5 \\ \hline \end{array}$ $\begin{array}{r} 8 \\ \times\ 6 \\ \hline \end{array}$ $\begin{array}{r} 8 \\ \times\ 3 \\ \hline \end{array}$

B. $\begin{array}{r} 9 \\ \times\ 3 \\ \hline \end{array}$ $\begin{array}{r} 9 \\ \times\ 9 \\ \hline \end{array}$ $\begin{array}{r} 7 \\ \times\ 8 \\ \hline \end{array}$ $\begin{array}{r} 2 \\ \times\ 9 \\ \hline \end{array}$ $\begin{array}{r} 4 \\ \times\ 8 \\ \hline \end{array}$

C. $\begin{array}{r} 9 \\ \times\ 8 \\ \hline \end{array}$ $\begin{array}{r} 9 \\ \times\ 0 \\ \hline \end{array}$ $\begin{array}{r} 2 \\ \times\ 8 \\ \hline \end{array}$ $\begin{array}{r} 8 \\ \times\ 8 \\ \hline \end{array}$ $\begin{array}{r} 6 \\ \times\ 9 \\ \hline \end{array}$

D. $\begin{array}{r} 9 \\ \times\ 4 \\ \hline \end{array}$ $\begin{array}{r} 9 \\ \times\ 7 \\ \hline \end{array}$ $\begin{array}{r} 1 \\ \times\ 9 \\ \hline \end{array}$ $\begin{array}{r} 8 \\ \times\ 4 \\ \hline \end{array}$ $\begin{array}{r} 0 \\ \times\ 8 \\ \hline \end{array}$

E. $\begin{array}{r} 3 \\ \times\ 9 \\ \hline \end{array}$ $\begin{array}{r} 5 \\ \times\ 8 \\ \hline \end{array}$ $\begin{array}{r} 7 \\ \times\ 9 \\ \hline \end{array}$ $\begin{array}{r} 1 \\ \times\ 8 \\ \hline \end{array}$ $\begin{array}{r} 5 \\ \times\ 9 \\ \hline \end{array}$

Circle the problem in Row E with the same product as 2 x 4.
Circle the problem in Row D with the same product as 3 x 3.
Circle the problem in Row C with the same product as 4 x 4.
Circle the problem in Row B with the same product as 6 x 3.
Circle the problem in Row A with the same product as 4 x 6.
Did you find your way to the top?

Scholastic

Multiply. Write the number word for each product in the puzzle. Don't forget the hyphens!

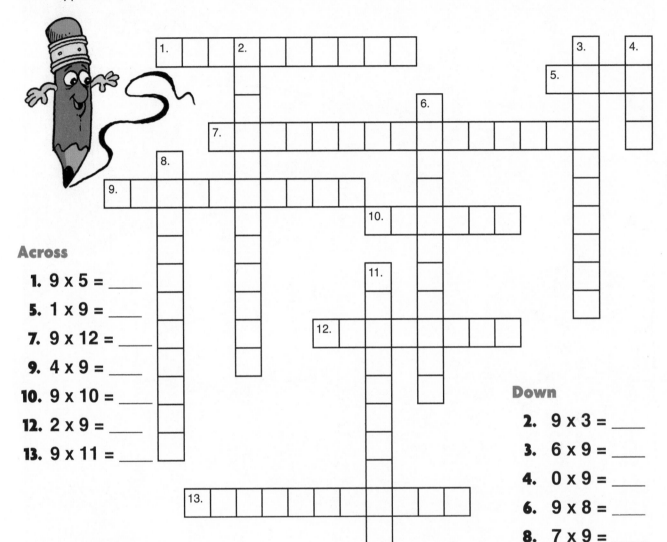

Across

1. 9 x 5 = _____

5. 1 x 9 = _____

7. 9 x 12 = _____

9. 4 x 9 = _____

10. 9 x 10 = _____

12. 2 x 9 = _____

13. 9 x 11 = _____

Down

2. 9 x 3 = _____

3. 6 x 9 = _____

4. 0 x 9 = _____

6. 9 x 8 = _____

8. 7 x 9 = _____

11. 9 x 9 = _____

 Justin just finished putting together a puzzle of a castle and wants to know how many pieces are in the puzzle. He knows he put together nine pieces every five minutes. If Justin worked for one hour, how many pieces does the puzzle have?

Scholastic

Multiply. Time yourself to see how fast you can finish the race.

51
x 5

24
x 2

92
x 4

63
x 2

14
x 2

12
x 4

73
x 3

83
x 2

44
x 2

61
x 4

51
x 2

42
x 3

FINISH

 Three race cars raced around the track. Each race car completed 32 laps. How many laps in all did the race cars complete?

Scholastic

Sometimes regrouping will be needed when multiplying with a two-digit number. Follow these steps to solve the problem.

1. Multiply the ones.
   Regroup if needed.

$7 \times 6 = 42$

2. Multiply the tens.
   Add the extra tens.

$4 \times 6 = 24$

$24 + 4 = 28$

Multiply. Remember to regroup.

A.   36
      x 4

   25
   x 5

   63
   x 7

B.   83
      x 8

   72
   x 6

   29
   x 4

   47
   x 6

   55
   x 7

C.   62
      x 5

   96
   x 2

   58
   x 5

   49
   x 3

   96
   x 4

Scholastic

Multiply. Regroup inside each leaf. Then use the code to answer the riddle below.

N. 34
x 6

C. 17
x 3

A. 46
x 4

H. 62
x 5

I. 53
x 6

B. 72
x 7

S. 28
x 4

K. 48
x 2

R. 18
x 6

B. 39
x 3

Where does a tree keep its money?

‾‾‾ ‾‾‾   ‾‾‾ ‾‾‾ ‾‾‾ ‾‾‾ ‾‾‾ ‾‾‾   ‾‾‾ ‾‾‾ ‾‾‾ ‾‾‾ ‾‾‾!
318 204   117 108 184 204 51 310   504 184 204 96 112

Scholastic

Multiply.

A. 314
  x   2

230
x   3

B. 432
  x   3

521
x   4

C. 604
  x   2

702
x   3

D. 723
  x   3

921
x   2

241
x   2

813
x   3

E. 112
  x   3

124
x   2

303
x   3

620
x   4

Scholastic

 The school science lab has 3 sets of test tubes. Each set has 112 tubes. How many are there in all?

Multiply. Then use a calculator to check your work.

A.
$$\begin{array}{r} 315 \\ \times \quad 9 \\ \hline \end{array}$$

B.
$$\begin{array}{r} 456 \\ \times \quad 4 \\ \hline \end{array}$$

C.
$$\begin{array}{r} 675 \\ \times \quad 5 \\ \hline \end{array}$$

D.
$$\begin{array}{r} 764 \\ \times \quad 7 \\ \hline \end{array}$$

E.
$$\begin{array}{r} 219 \\ \times \quad 8 \\ \hline \end{array}$$

F.
$$\begin{array}{r} 968 \\ \times \quad 3 \\ \hline \end{array}$$

G.
$$\begin{array}{r} 391 \\ \times \quad 4 \\ \hline \end{array}$$

H.
$$\begin{array}{r} 532 \\ \times \quad 6 \\ \hline \end{array}$$

I.
$$\begin{array}{r} 808 \\ \times \quad 4 \\ \hline \end{array}$$

J.
$$\begin{array}{r} 270 \\ \times \quad 9 \\ \hline \end{array}$$

 On another piece of paper, write five multiplication problems with a three-digit number. Multiply. Check each answer with a calculator.

Scholastic

Write a number sentence for each problem. Solve.

A. Connor's dog, Barky, made 3 holes in the backyard. Connor's dad had to fill each hole with 78 scoops of dirt. How many scoops did his dad need in all?

B. Barky got into Steve's closet. He chewed up 8 pairs of shoes. How many shoes did he chew altogether?

C. Adrienne went to the store to buy doggie treats. She bought 6 boxes of doggie treats. Each box has 48 treats. How many treats in all did Adrienne buy?

D. Terri took Barky to the vet for 3 shots. Each shot cost $2.65. How much money did Terri pay the vet?

E. Max's job is to keep Barky's water bowl full. If he fills it 3 times a day for 24 days, how many times did he fill the bowl altogether?

F. Barky runs around the block 4 times every day. How many times does he run around the block in 5 days?

 On another piece of paper, write your own Barky word problem. Solve.

Scholastic

To make easy numbers, first multiply numbers that result in either 10 or 100. Then multiply the rest of the numbers in the equation. For example:

2 x 9 x 5

= (2 x 5) x 9

= 10 x 9

= 90

Make easy numbers to solve the problems below. Draw a line to match the problem to the answer.

1.	2 x 9 x 5 =	**a.**	300
2.	10 x 3 x 10 =	**b.**	800
3.	5 x 13 x 2 =	**c.**	250
4.	2 x 5 x 37 =	**d.**	600
5.	50 x 7 x 2 =	**e.**	700
6.	4 x 8 x 25 =	**f.**	90
7.	50 x 9 x 2 =	**g.**	500
8.	5 x 5 x 5 x 2 =	**h.**	370
9.	2 x 2 x 5 x 3 =	**i.**	60
10.	2 x 10 x 5 x 5 =	**j.**	900
11.	1 x 2 x 4 x 2 x 5 =	**k.**	130
12.	2 x 3 x 5 x 4 x 5 =	**l.**	80

Scholastic

To divide means to make equal groups. The total number being divided is called the **dividend**. *The number of groups the total is to be divided into is called the* **divisor**. *The answer is called the* **quotient**.   *6 ÷ 2 = 3*

total number (dividend–6)	*number of groups (divisor–2)*	*number in each group (quotient–3)*

The Bird House has 10 birds in all. The zookeeper wants to put the birds into the 5 new cages he bought. How many birds will he put in each cage?

Solve this problem by drawing a picture. Draw the number of birds you think need to go in each cage. (Hint: Each cage must have the same number of birds.) Then complete the number sentence.

Total Number of Birds	Number of Cages	Number of Birds in Each Cage
_____ ÷	5	= _____

What if the zookeeper only had 2 cages? How many birds would go in each cage? Draw a picture. Then write a number sentence.

_____ ÷ _____ = _____

Scholastic

Draw a circle around the correct number of stars to show each division problem. Complete each number sentence.

A. 8 ÷ 2 = ___4___

B. 6 ÷ 3 = _____

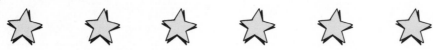

C. 12 ÷ 3 = _____

D. 10 ÷ 2 = _____

E. 18 ÷ 3 = _____

F. 9 ÷ 3 = _____

G. 16 ÷ 2 = _____

H. 15 ÷ 3 = _____

Scholastic

Divide.

A. 6 ÷ 2 = _____   9 ÷ 3 = _____   10 ÷ 2 = _____

B. 12 ÷ 3 = _____   14 ÷ 2 = _____   8 ÷ 2 = _____

C. 2 ÷ 2 = _____   18 ÷ 3 = _____   24 ÷ 3 = _____

D. 2) 12   3) 21

E. 3) 6   3) 3

F. 3) 15   2) 16

G. There are 18 aliens ready to board their spaceships. If 6 aliens get on each spaceship, how many spaceships do they need? Draw a picture to show the problem. Then write a number sentence to solve the problem.

Scholastic

Divide.

A.   30 ÷ 5 = _____   32 ÷ 4 = _____   45 ÷ 5 = _____   5 ÷ 5 = _____

B.   36 ÷ 4 = _____   20 ÷ 4 = _____   25 ÷ 5 = _____   28 ÷ 4 = _____

C.   5 ⟌ 10   4 ⟌ 16   5 ⟌ 40   5 ⟌ 45   4 ⟌ 20

D.   4 ⟌ 12   5 ⟌ 35   4 ⟌ 8   5 ⟌ 15   4 ⟌ 24

E.   Lisa tied a total of 12 ribbons on her kites. If she tied 4 ribbons on each kite, how many kites does Lisa have?

There were 36 people flying kites in the park. There were an equal number of yellow, green, orange, and blue kites. How many kites are there of each color?

You can use a number line to help divide. Count back in equal groups to 0.

$28 \div 4 = 7$

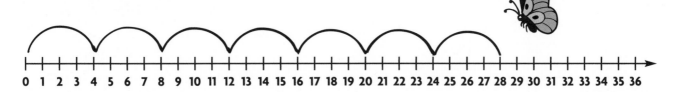

Divide. Use the number line to help you.

A. 4) 16   4) 36   4) 4   4) 24

B. 4) 20   4) 12   4) 32   4) 8

C. $32 \div 4 =$ _____ $16 \div 4 =$ _____ $20 \div 4 =$ _____

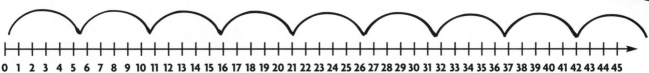

Divide. Use the number line to help you.

D. 5) 15   5) 5   5) 40   5) 45

E. 5) 25   5) 10   5) 20   5) 10

Scholastic

Divide.

A. 42 ÷ 7 = _____   54 ÷ 6 = _____   36 ÷ 6 = _____

B. 24 ÷ 6 = _____   63 ÷ 7 = _____   48 ÷ 6 = _____

C. 14 ÷ 7 = _____   56 ÷ 7 = _____   28 ÷ 7 = _____

D. 49 ÷ 7 = _____   60 ÷ 6 = _____   42 ÷ 6 = _____

E. Fifty-six students went on a field trip to the zoo. They traveled in 7 vans. How many students were in each van?

F. When the students went to the monkey house, they found it was divided into 6 rooms. The same number of monkeys were in each room. There were 24 monkeys in all. How many monkeys were in each room?

MONKEY HOUSE

Scholastic

Circle the skates and helmets with the correct quotient.

2. $8\overline{)72}$ → 8

3. $9\overline{)36}$ → 4

4. $56 \div 8 =$ ___6___

1. $90 \div 9 =$ ___10___

5. $24 \div 8 =$ ___3___

6. $9\overline{)45}$ → 5

8. $48 \div 8 =$ ___8___

7. $8\overline{)32}$ → 4

9. $8\overline{)40}$ → 4

10. $9\overline{)18}$ → 2

12. $8\overline{)64}$ → 8

11. $63 \div 9 =$ ___7___

13. $80 \div 8 =$ ___11___

14. $81 \div 9 =$ ___9___

Peter wants to skate 18 miles in the next 9 days. If he skates an equal number of miles each day, how many miles will he need to skate each day?

Scholastic

Divide to find the answers on each runner's path to the finish line.

$81 \div 9 =$ _____

$16 \div 8 =$ _____

$32 \div 8 =$ _____

$45 \div 9 =$ _____

$8 \overline{)40}$

$9 \overline{)63}$

$64 \div 8 =$ _____

$18 \div 9 =$ _____

$27 \div 9 =$ _____

$9 \div 9 =$ _____

$9 \overline{)36}$

$8 \overline{)24}$

FINISH

$8 \div 0 =$ _____

$56 \div 8 =$ _____

$9 \overline{)54}$

$8 \overline{)72}$

$48 \div 8 =$ _____

$80 \div 8 =$ _____

 Last week in track practice, Andy ran 36 miles. He ran the same number of miles on each of the 4 days. How many miles did he run each day?

Scholastic

*Sometimes when you try to divide a number into equal groups, part of the number is left over. This is called the **remainder**. Use these steps to find the remainder.*

1.
$$5 \overline{)16}$$

Think: 5 x ___ is the closest to 16?

2.
$$5 \overline{)\begin{array}{r} 3 \\ 16 \\ -15 \\ \hline 1 \end{array}}$$

3.
$$5 \overline{)\begin{array}{r} 3\ R\ 1 \\ 16 \\ -15 \\ \hline 1 \end{array}}$$

There are 5 groups of 3 with 1 left over.

Divide.

A.
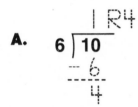
$$6 \overline{)\begin{array}{r} 1\ R4 \\ 10 \\ -6 \\ \hline 4 \end{array}}$$

$2 \overline{)9}$

B. $3 \overline{)20}$ $2 \overline{)19}$ $6 \overline{)47}$ $6 \overline{)41}$

C. $7 \overline{)51}$ $2 \overline{)15}$ $3 \overline{)22}$ $7 \overline{)48}$

D. $2 \overline{)11}$ $4 \overline{)26}$ $6 \overline{)19}$ $5 \overline{)27}$

 Louie jumps hurdles for his track meet. He jumps the same number in each race. In his last 6 races, he jumped 36 hurdles. How many hurdles did he jump each day?

Scholastic

Divide.

A. $5 \overline{)41}$ $6 \overline{)52}$ $3 \overline{)19}$ $8 \overline{)74}$

B. $4 \overline{)29}$ $2 \overline{)13}$ $7 \overline{)38}$ $9 \overline{)46}$

C. $5 \overline{)21}$ $6 \overline{)31}$ $3 \overline{)26}$ $8 \overline{)57}$

D. $4 \overline{)14}$ $2 \overline{)7}$ $7 \overline{)65}$ $9 \overline{)51}$

E. $3 \overline{)13}$ $6 \overline{)39}$ $5 \overline{)14}$ $8 \overline{)50}$

 Candy's mom bought 56 apples to make 8 pies. If she used an equal number of apples in each pie, how many apples did she use in each pie? Solve on another piece of paper.

Scholastic

*Remember: The **quotient** tells how many
equal groups you can make. The **remainder**
tells how many are left over.*

Divide. Answer each question.

A. A clothing-store clerk has 14
sweaters. He wants to put them
in equal stacks on 3 shelves.
How many sweaters will be in
each stack?

B. Mary has 57¢. She wants to buy
candy canes that cost 9¢
each. How many candy canes
can she buy?

C. Rosa needs to bake 71 cookies.
Each cookie sheet holds 8
cookies. How many cookies are
on the unfilled cookie sheet?

D. There are 17 cars waiting to be
parked, but not enough parking
spaces. There are an equal
number of parking spots on 3
different levels. How many cars
will not find a parking spot?

E. Luis is putting 74 cans into
cartons. Each carton holds 8
cans. How many cans will be in
the unfilled carton?

F. Don bought 85 crates of
flowers. He separates them into
groups of 9. How many equal
groups did he have?

Scholastic

Use these steps when dividing with greater dividends.

1. Divide the tens digit in the dividend by the divisor. Write the answer above the tens digit.

2. Multiply the partial quotient by the divisor. Write the answer below the tens digit. Subtract. Bring down the ones digit.

3. Divide the ones digit by the divisor. Write the answer above the ones digit. Multiply. Subtract.

$$\begin{array}{r} 2 \\ 4\overline{)84} \end{array}$$

$$\begin{array}{r} 2 \\ 4\overline{)84} \\ -8\downarrow \\ \hline 04 \end{array}$$

$$\begin{array}{r} 21 \\ 4\overline{)84} \\ -8\downarrow \\ \hline 04 \\ -4 \\ \hline 0 \end{array}$$

Divide.

A.

$3\overline{)66}$ $2\overline{)48}$ $3\overline{)93}$ $3\overline{)39}$

B.

$3\overline{)96}$ $3\overline{)63}$ $2\overline{)68}$ $9\overline{)90}$

C.

$3\overline{)99}$ $3\overline{)69}$ $2\overline{)80}$ $5\overline{)55}$

Scholastic

Remember to follow each step when dividing larger numbers.

1. Divide the tens digit by the divisor. Multiply. Subtract.

$$
\begin{array}{r}
1 \\
3\overline{)45} \\
-3 \\
\hline
1
\end{array}
$$

2. Bring down the ones digit. Divide this number by the divisor.

$$
\begin{array}{r}
15 \\
3\overline{)45} \\
-3\downarrow \\
\hline
15
\end{array}
$$

3. Multiply. Subtract.

$$
\begin{array}{r}
15 \\
3\overline{)45} \\
-3\downarrow \\
\hline
15 \\
-15 \\
\hline
0
\end{array}
$$

Divide.

A.

$2\overline{)58}$ $5\overline{)85}$ $6\overline{)72}$ $5\overline{)90}$

B.

$3\overline{)48}$ $8\overline{)96}$ $2\overline{)74}$ $4\overline{)92}$

C.

$6\overline{)78}$ $4\overline{)76}$ $5\overline{)65}$ $4\overline{)60}$

Scholastic

 Andrew has 87 marbles. He divides them into 3 bags. How many marbles are in each bag? Solve. Then circle the problem above with the same quotient.

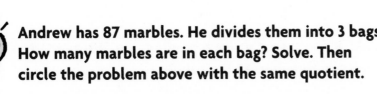

Remember that multiplication and division are related. Multiplying the quotient by the divisor will tell you the dividend.

Hi! Aren't we related?

You bet! When you multiply us, our missing product is the missing dividend!

Write each missing dividend.

A. _____ ÷ 9 = 7   _____ ÷ 4 = 6   _____ ÷ 6 = 6   _____ ÷ 5 = 7

B. _____ ÷ 3 = 3   _____ ÷ 2 = 9   _____ ÷ 8 = 6   _____ ÷ 9 = 9

C. _____ ÷ 4 = 8   _____ ÷ 3 = 7   _____ ÷ 2 = 8   _____ ÷ 6 = 3

D. _____ ÷ 8 = 8   _____ ÷ 1 = 9   _____ ÷ 5 = 6   _____ ÷ 7 = 1

Are we missing?

E. _____ ÷ 4 = 40   _____ ÷ 3 = 30   _____ ÷ 3 = 100

F. _____ ÷ 7 = 60   _____ ÷ 5 = 60   _____ ÷ 2 = 40

 At our family reunion picnic, 8 people sat at each picnic table. We needed 16 tables. How many people altogether were at the reunion?

Scholastic

Decide whether to multiply
or divide. Solve.

A. Ellen baked 75 cookies in 3
hours. Joe baked 96 cookies in 4
hours. Who baked the most
cookies per hour?

B. James pitched 18 times in each
inning of the ball game. How
many times did he pitch in the 9
innings?

C. Lana bought 4 20-ounce sodas.
How many 4-ounce servings
can she give her party guests?

D. Cory's mom sent him to the store
for eggs. He bought 4 cartons of
a dozen eggs. How many eggs
did he purchase in all?

E. Maria made bracelets for her
friends. She put 9 beads on
each. She had 81 beads. How
many bracelets did she make?

F. It costs 50¢ per hour to park at
the beach. How much did it cost
David's parents to park for 8
hours?

Scholastic

Solve each problem by breaking up numbers. Then regroup the numbers for easier multiplication and division. Look at the multiplication and division examples here.

Examples:

4×12	3×56	$36 \div 4$	$56 \div 4$
$= 4 \times (10 + 2)$	$= 3 \times (50 + 6)$	$= (20 + 16) \div 4$	$= (40 + 16) \div 4$
$= (4 \times 10) + (4 \times 2)$	$= (3 \times 50) + (3 \times 6)$	$= (20 \div 4) + (16 \div 4)$	$= (40 \div 4) + (16 \div 4)$
$= 40 + 8$	$= 150 + 18$	$= 5 + 4$	$= 10 + 4$
$= 48$	$= 168$	$= 9$	$= 14$

1. $3 \times 12 =$ _____

2. $5 \times 31 =$ _____

3. $4 \times 62 =$ _____

4. $2 \times 43 =$ _____

5. $4 \times 24 =$ _____

6. $3 \times 18 =$ _____

7. $5 \times 36 =$ _____

8. $8 \times 13 =$ _____

9. $7 \times 24 =$ _____

10. $6 \times 36 =$ _____

11. $24 \div 4 =$ _____

12. $35 \div 5 =$ _____

13. $48 \div 8 =$ _____

14. $56 \div 7 =$ _____

15. $26 \div 2 =$ _____

16. $48 \div 4 =$ _____

17. $75 \div 5 =$ _____

18. $96 \div 8 =$ _____

19. $64 \div 4 =$ _____

20. $60 \div 5 =$ _____

Write About It

Explain what shortcuts you used for one of the problems.

_____

_____

Scholastic

Multiplication & Division Practice Test

Fill in the bubble next to the correct answer.

1.
$$\begin{array}{r} 333 \\ \times\ \ 3 \\ \hline \end{array}$$

○ **A** 999

○ **B** 989

○ **C** 987

○ **D** 936

3.
$$\begin{array}{r} 125 \\ \times\ \ 7 \\ \hline \end{array}$$

○ **A** 875

○ **B** 775

○ **C** 735

○ **D** 835

2. Find the missing factor.

$4 \times \underline{\hspace{1cm}} = 12$

○ **F** 3

○ **G** 4

○ **H** 5

○ **J** 6

4. Find the missing factor.

$\underline{\hspace{1cm}} \times 9 = 18$

○ **F** 4

○ **G** 2

○ **H** 3

○ **J** 5

Multiplication & Division Practice Test

Fill in the bubble next to the correct answer.

5. $65 \div 5 =$

    ◯ **A**   11

    ◯ **B**   12

    ◯ **C**   13

    ◯ **D**   14

7. $8 \overline{)16}$

    ◯ **A**   5

    ◯ **B**   4

    ◯ **C**   3

    ◯ **D**   2

6. $16 \div 4 =$

    ◯ **F**   1

    ◯ **G**   3

    ◯ **H**   4

    ◯ **J**   5

8. $5 \overline{)40}$

    ◯ **F**   6

    ◯ **G**   7

    ◯ **H**   8

    ◯ **J**   9

Scholastic

Multiplication & Division Practice Test

Fill in the bubble next to the correct answer.

9. Fifty-six students went on a field trip to the zoo. They traveled in 7 vans. How many students were in each van?

- ○ **A** 7
- ○ **B** 8
- ○ **C** 5
- ○ **D** 9

10. When the students went to the snake house they found 5 cages. There were 4 snakes in each cage. How many snakes were in the snake house?

- ○ **F** 30
- ○ **G** 25
- ○ **H** 20
- ○ **J** 35

11. When the students went to the monkey house, they found it was divided into 5 rooms. The same number of monkeys were in each room. There were 30 monkeys in all. How many monkeys were in each room?

- ○ **A** 6
- ○ **B** 7
- ○ **C** 3
- ○ **D** 5

12. When the students went to see the lions, they saw 3 separate cages. There were 2 lions in each cage. How many lions were in the lion house?

- ○ **F** 6
- ○ **G** 3
- ○ **H** 2
- ○ **J** 4

Scholastic

Fractions & Graphs

If your child likes to cook, he or she will find it very helpful to understand fractions. Most recipes have ingredients that are measured in fractions.

Graphs are important to understand because they can show a great deal of information in a way that is fun and easy to read.

What to Do

The activities in this section introduce your child to concepts related to fractions and graphing. Read the directions together. Have your child complete the activity. Then together, review his or her work. Remember, answers, if you need them, have been provided at the back of the book. Reward your child with a sticker for work that is well done!

Keep On Going!

Use food to reinforce fractions. For example, have your child count the number of slices of pizza in the pan. Ask questions such as "Dad ate 3 pieces of pizza. What fraction describes the amount of pizza he ate?" ($\frac{3}{8}$) Continue asking questions using other family members. Challenge your child to use the information to make a bar graph. Label the vertical axis 1–8. Label the horizontal axis with the names of the family members. Bet you didn't know you could eat math!

Wash your hands, then gather the recipe ingredients and equipment listed below. To prepare the peanut butter-oatmeal drops, simply mix the ingredients together, roll the dough into balls, and place the balls on the wax paper. Chill the finished drops for about an hour, then enjoy your tasty "fractions" with family or friends!

NO-BAKE PEANUT BUTTER-OATMEAL DROPS
(makes about 30 1-inch drops)

 cup peanut butter (smooth or crunchy)

 cup corn syrup

cup confectioner's sugar

cup powdered milk

cup uncooked oatmeal

Mix all the ingredients together. Roll into balls. Chill for about one hour. Then eat!

Now try these fraction pictures. Can you write the fraction each picture shows?

1.   _____

2. 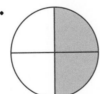 _____

3. 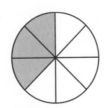 _____

4. 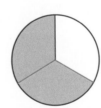 _____

5. 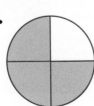 _____

6. 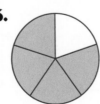 _____

7. 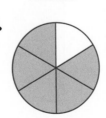 _____

8. 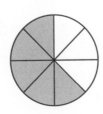 _____

Scholastic

Write a fraction for the section of the flag next to the arrow.

1. PANAMA

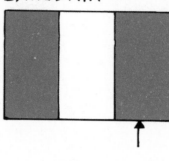

_____

2. NIGERIA

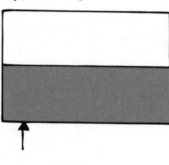

_____

3. TAIWAN

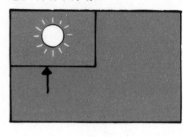

_____

4. MALTA

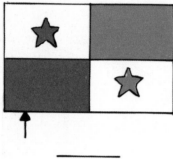

_____

5. POLAND

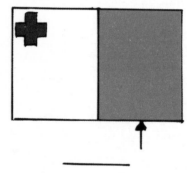

_____

6. MAURITIUS

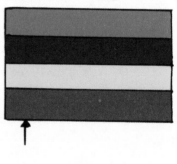

_____

7. RUSSIA

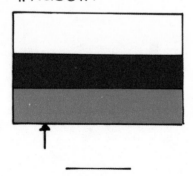

_____

8. CHILE

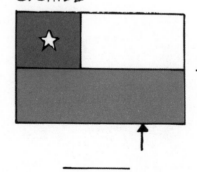

_____

9. MALAWI

_____

Scholastic

Choose 2 colors for each bunch of flowers. Color some
of the flowers one color. Color the rest of the flowers
the other color. Write a fraction to tell how many
flowers there are of each color.

1.

$\dfrac{}{8}$ are ☐

$\dfrac{}{8}$ are ☐

2.

$\dfrac{}{6}$ are ☐

$\dfrac{}{6}$ are ☐

3.

$\dfrac{}{5}$ are ☐

$\dfrac{}{5}$ are ☐

Scholastic

To reduce a fraction to lowest terms, find a common factor that will divide into both the numerator and the denominator. The factor 2 will work. The factor 4, however, is better. When the only factor is 1, the fraction has been reduced to lowest terms.

$$\frac{4 \div 2}{8 \div 2} = \frac{2}{4}$$

Divide by 2. Can you divide again? Yes!

$$\frac{2 \div 2}{4 \div 2} = \frac{1}{2}$$

Divide by 2. Can you divide again? No!

$$\frac{4 \div 4}{8 \div 4} = \frac{1}{2}$$

Divide by 4. Can you divide again? No!

Choose the greatest common factor for each fraction from the box. Divide and reduce to lowest terms.

A. $\boxed{3 \quad 2 \quad 4}$ $\dfrac{2 \div \square}{4 \div \square} =$

B. $\boxed{6 \quad 3 \quad 2}$ $\dfrac{6 \div \square}{9 \div \square} =$

C. $\boxed{4 \quad 5 \quad 2}$ $\dfrac{5 \div \square}{10 \div \square} =$

D. $\boxed{3 \quad 5 \quad 2}$ $\dfrac{10 \div \square}{15 \div \square} =$

E. $\boxed{2 \quad 4 \quad 6}$ $\dfrac{4 \div \square}{8 \div \square} =$

F. $\boxed{8 \quad 2 \quad 10}$ $\dfrac{10 \div \square}{12 \div \square} =$

G. $\boxed{2 \quad 8 \quad 3}$ $\dfrac{3 \div \square}{6 \div \square} =$

H. $\boxed{4 \quad 6 \quad 3}$ $\dfrac{3 \div \square}{9 \div \square} =$

I. $\boxed{2 \quad 7 \quad 4}$ $\dfrac{7 \div \square}{14 \div \square} =$

J. $\boxed{2 \quad 6 \quad 3}$ $\dfrac{6 \div \square}{8 \div \square} =$

K. $\boxed{5 \quad 10 \quad 3}$ $\dfrac{5 \div \square}{15 \div \square} =$

L. $\boxed{6 \quad 8 \quad 4}$ $\dfrac{4 \div \square}{16 \div \square} =$

Scholastic

Follow the coordinates to the correct box, then draw in the underlined treasures on this treasure map.

C3 A <u>jeweled crown</u> sparkles.
B1 A <u>ruby necklace</u> can be found.
C5 A <u>golden cup</u> awaits you.
D4 An <u>X</u> marks the spot!
A4 A <u>wooden treasure chest</u> you'll find.
E1 A <u>silvery sword</u> lies here.

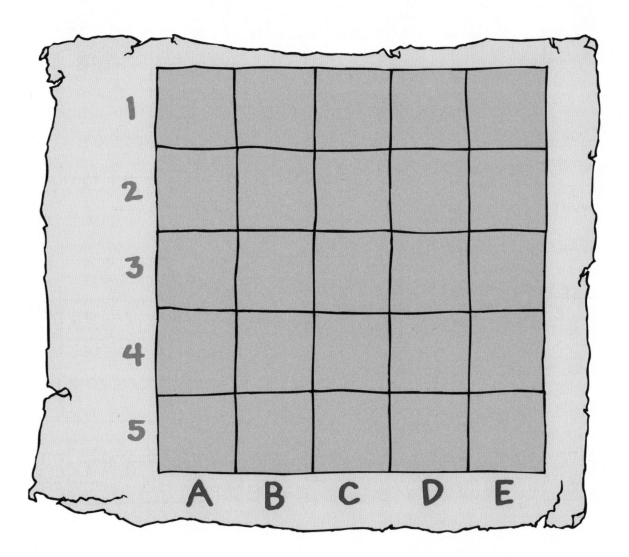

Scholastic

A line graph shows how something changes over time. This line graph shows temperature changes during a year in New York City. Use the graph to answer the questions below.

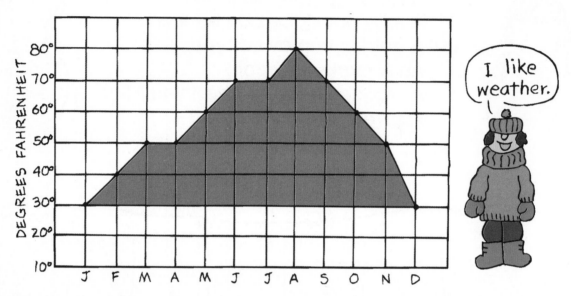

SUGGESTION: SHORTEN THE NAMES, LIKE JAN, FEB, AUG, SEP, OCT, NOV.

1. WHAT 2 MONTHS WERE THE COLDEST? _____

2. WHAT WAS THE TEMPERATURE OF THE HOTTEST MONTH? _____

3. WHAT MONTHS WERE 70°? _____

4. ANY TEMPERATURE CHANGE BETWEEN JAN. AND FEB.? _____

5. WAS THE TEMPERATURE EVER WARMER THAN AUGUST? _____

6. DID IT BECOME COLDER OR WARMER IN JUNE? _____

7. DID THE TEMPERATURE RISE OR FALL IN OCTOBER? _____

8. WHAT MONTH IS THE 5th MONTH? _____

9. HOW MANY DEGREES BETWEEN 40° AND 80°? _____

Scholastic

A bar graph shows information. This bar graph shows the speeds of animals in miles per hour. Use the graph to answer the questions.

WHICH ANIMAL IS...

1. THE FASTEST?

_____

2. THE SLOWEST?

_____

3. GOING 40 mph?

_____

4. 20 mph FASTER THAN A CAT?

_____

5. HOW MANY 4-FOOTED ANIMALS ARE LISTED?

_____

DO THE BARS SHOW...

6. ANIMAL NAMES AND mph?

_____

7. SPEED OR WEIGHT?

_____

8. INFORMATION ABOUT TIGERS?

_____

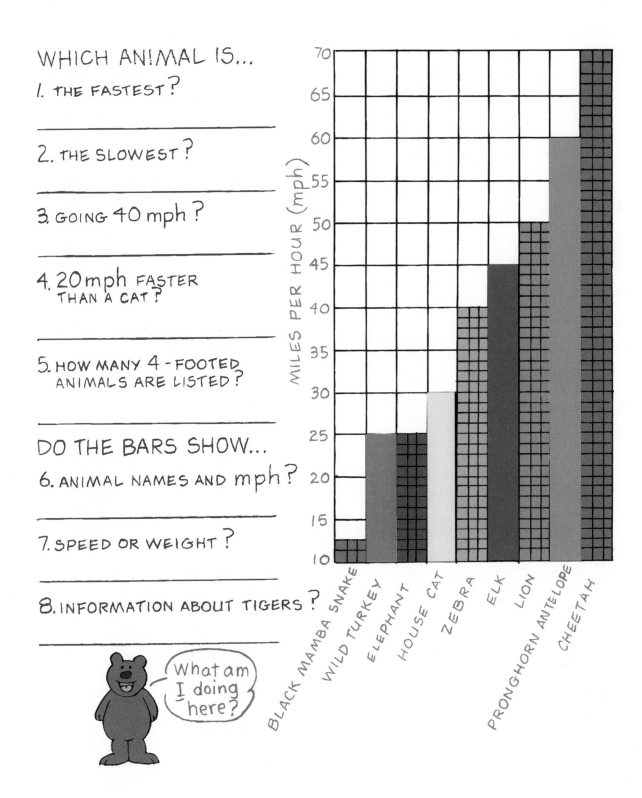

1. Solve each multiplication problem. Example problems have been done for you.

2. In the example problems, the numbers **4** and **8** are called a number pair. We write (4, 8).

3. Look at the graph on page 251. Graph the number pairs in the example. Start at 0. Go across to the number **4** and up to the number **8**. Plot the point.

4. Plot the point for each number pair, in order. Then use a straightedge to connect the points in the order you plotted them. After the word STOP, start a new line. Can you solve the riddle?

	X →	Y ↑
	1 x 4 = 4	2 x 4 = 8 (Example)
1.	11 x 4 = _____	2 x 4 = _____
2.	4 x 11 = _____	9 x 4 = _____
3.	1 x 4 = _____	4 x 9 = _____
4.	4 x 1 = _____	4 x 2 = _____
5.	4 x 2 = _____	4 x 3 = _____
6.	3 x 4 = _____	4 x 4 = _____
7.	4 x 4 = _____	4 x 5 = _____
8.	5 x 4 = _____	6 x 4 = _____ STOP
9.	4 x 1 = _____	9 x 4 = _____
10.	4 x 6 = _____	4 x 5 = _____
11.	11 x 4 = _____	4 x 9 = _____ STOP
12.	4 x 7 = _____	6 x 4 = _____
13.	4 x 8 = _____	5 x 4 = _____
14.	9 x 4 = _____	4 x 4 = _____
15.	10 x 4 = _____	4 x 3 = _____
16.	4 x 11 = _____	4 x 2 = _____

EXTRA CHALLENGE!

What letter never gets put in an envelope? Solve the riddle by replacing the answers to the problems with the alphabet code.

E = 12   B = 16   A = 20

4 x 5 = ____ ☐   4 x 4 = ____ ☐   4 x 3 = ____ ☐   3 x 4 = ____ ☐

Scholastic

I start with an *e* and have only one letter. What am I? _____

To find out the answer, solve the problems on page 250. Then plot the number pairs and connect the points. The picture you make will help you solve the riddle. (The answer is upside down at the bottom of this page.)

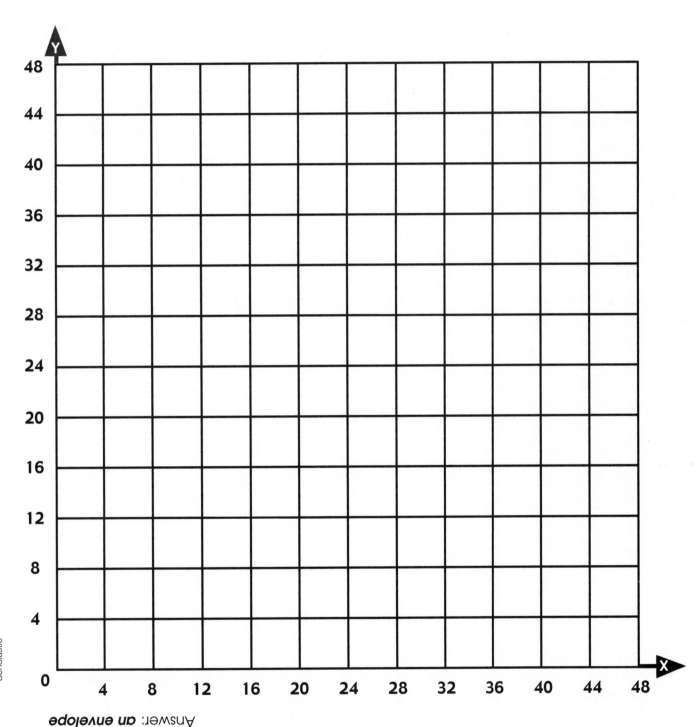

Answer: an envelope

Scholastic

1. Solve each division problem. Example problems have been done for you.

2. In the example problems, the numbers **2** and **3** are called a number pair. We write (2, 3).

3. Look at the graph on page 253. Graph the number pair in the example. Start at 0. Go across to the number **2** and up to the number **3**. Plot the point.

4. Plot the point for each number pair, in order. Then use a straightedge to connect the points in the order you plotted them. After the word STOP, start a new line. Can you solve the riddle?

	X $\longrightarrow$	Y $\uparrow$
	18 ÷ 9 = 2	27 ÷ 9 = 3 (Example)
1.	36 ÷ 9 = _____	9 ÷ 9 = _____
2.	81 ÷ 9 = _____	9 ÷ 9 = _____
3.	81 ÷ 9 = _____	27 ÷ 9 = _____
4.	18 ÷ 9 = _____	27 ÷ 9 = _____ STOP
5.	72 ÷ 9 = _____	27 ÷ 9 = _____
6.	72 ÷ 9 = _____	45 ÷ 9 = _____
7.	72 ÷ 9 = _____	81 ÷ 9 = _____
8.	54 ÷ 9 = _____	81 ÷ 9 = _____
9.	54 ÷ 9 = _____	99 ÷ 9 = _____
10.	63 ÷ 9 = _____	90 ÷ 9 = _____
11.	54 ÷ 9 = _____	81 ÷ 9 = _____
12.	36 ÷ 9 = _____	81 ÷ 9 = _____
13.	36 ÷ 9 = _____	27 ÷ 9 = _____

EXTRA CHALLENGE!

Captain Crook was a pirate who was loved by none and feared by all. He hid his chests of gold, silver, and jewels somewhere in the Caribbean. When he died, this note was found tucked in the bottom of Captain Crook's boot. Replace each division problem in the note with the answer and read the message.

The (36 ÷ 9 tune) is aboard the ship called (36 ÷ 9 got 90 ÷ 9) Bounty in Red Hook Bay!

Scholastic

The older I get, the smaller I become. What am I? _____

To find out the answer, solve the problems on page 252. Then plot the number pairs and connect the points. The picture you make will help you solve the riddle. (The answer is upside down at the bottom of this page.)

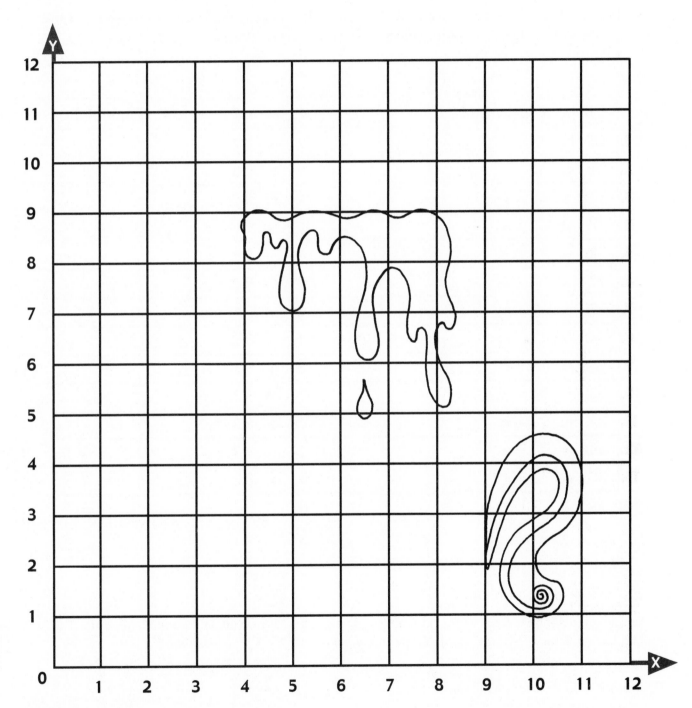

Answer: a candle

Scholastic

1. Solve each multiplication problem. Example problems have been done for you.

2. In the example problems, the numbers **42** and **14** are called a number pair. We write (42, 14).

3. Look at the graph on page 255. Graph the number pairs in the example. Start at 0. Go across to the number **42** and up to the number **14**. Plot the point.

4. Plot the point for each number pair, in order. Then use a straightedge to connect the points in the order you plotted them. After the word STOP, start a new line. Can you solve the riddle?

	X ⟶	Y ↑
	6 x 7 = 42	2 x 7 = 14 (Example)
1.	7 x 11 = _____	7 x 7 = _____
2.	7 x 10 = _____	7 x 9 = _____
3.	9 x 7 = _____	11 x 7 = _____
4.	7 x 7 = _____	10 x 7 = _____
5.	5 x 7 = _____	7 x 9 = _____
6.	7 x 6 = _____	7 x 2 = _____ STOP
7.	7 x 2 = _____	7 x 1 = _____
8.	3 x 7 = _____	1 x 7 = _____
9.	7 x 3 = _____	3 x 7 = _____
10.	7 x 4 = _____	7 x 3 = _____
11.	4 x 7 = _____	7 x 2 = _____
12.	3 x 7 = _____	2 x 7 = _____
13.	7 x 2 = _____	7 x 2 = _____
14.	2 x 7 = _____	1 x 7 = _____

EXTRA CHALLENGE!

Which kite belongs to Pauley? Read the following clues and draw a circle around Pauley's kite. The number on Pauley's kite is a multiple of 7. It is greater than 7 x 3. It is less than 7 x 6.

 21  15  63  25 35 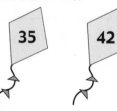 42

Scholastic

**I like to fly in the bright blue sky, soaring ever higher—until I meet a wire!
What am I?** _____

To find out the answer, solve the problems on page 254. Then plot the number pairs and connect the points. The picture you make will help you solve the riddle. (The answer is upside down at the bottom of this page.)

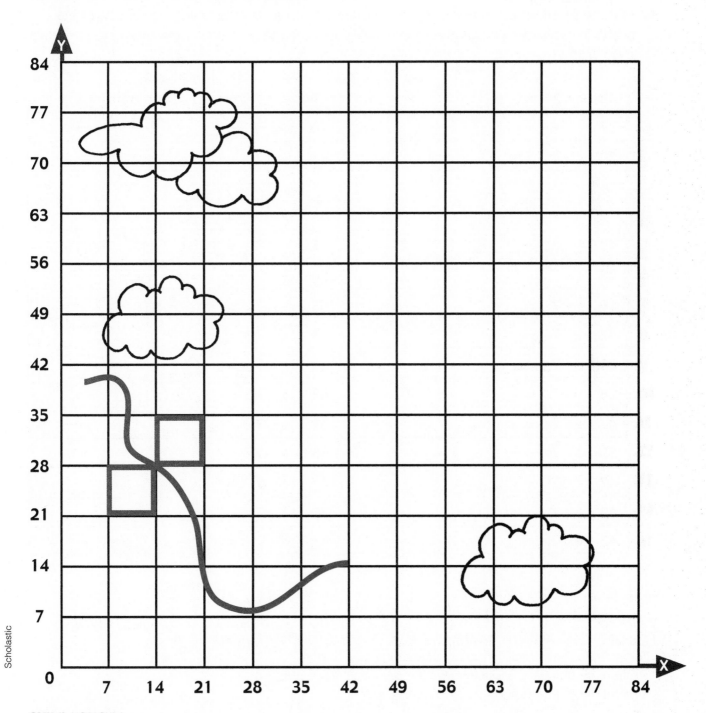

Answer: **a kite**

1. Solve each division problem. Example problems have been done for you.
2. In the example problems, the numbers **6** and **1** are called a number pair. We write (6,1).
3. Look at the graph on page 257. Graph the number pair in the example. Start at 0. Go across to the number **6** and up to the number **1**. Plot the point.
4. Plot the point for each number pair, in order. Then use a straightedge to connect the points in the order you plotted them. After the word STOP, start a new line. Can you solve the riddle?

X → Y ↑

	42 ÷ 7 = 6	7 ÷ 7 = 1 (Example)
1.	77 ÷ 7 = _____	56 ÷ 7 = _____
2.	70 ÷ 7 = _____	63 ÷ 7 = _____
3.	14 ÷ 7 = _____	63 ÷ 7 = _____
4.	7 ÷ 7 = _____	56 ÷ 7 = _____
5.	42 ÷ 7 = _____	7 ÷ 7 = _____
6.	63 ÷ 7 = _____	56 ÷ 7 = _____
7.	56 ÷ 7 = _____	63 ÷ 7 = _____ STOP
8.	42 ÷ 7 = _____	7 ÷ 7 = _____
9.	21 ÷ 7 = _____	56 ÷ 7 = _____
10.	28 ÷ 7 = _____	63 ÷ 7 = _____ STOP
11.	42 ÷ 7 = _____	63 ÷ 7 = _____
12.	35 ÷ 7 = _____	56 ÷ 7 = _____
13.	42 ÷ 7 = _____	7 ÷ 7 = _____
14.	49 ÷ 7 = _____	56 ÷ 7 = _____
15.	42 ÷ 7 = _____	63 ÷ 7 = _____

EXTRA CHALLENGE!

Today is Amina's birthday. Use the information below to figure out how old she is.

Today Amina is twice as old as her little brother.

Amina's brother Zack is less than 8 but more than 5 years old.

Both of the children's ages are even numbers.

Amina is _____ years old.

Scholastic

What did the baseball player buy his wife for her birthday? _____

To find out the answer, solve the problems on page 256. Then plot the number pairs and connect the points. The picture you make will help you solve the riddle. (The answer is upside down at the bottom of this page.)

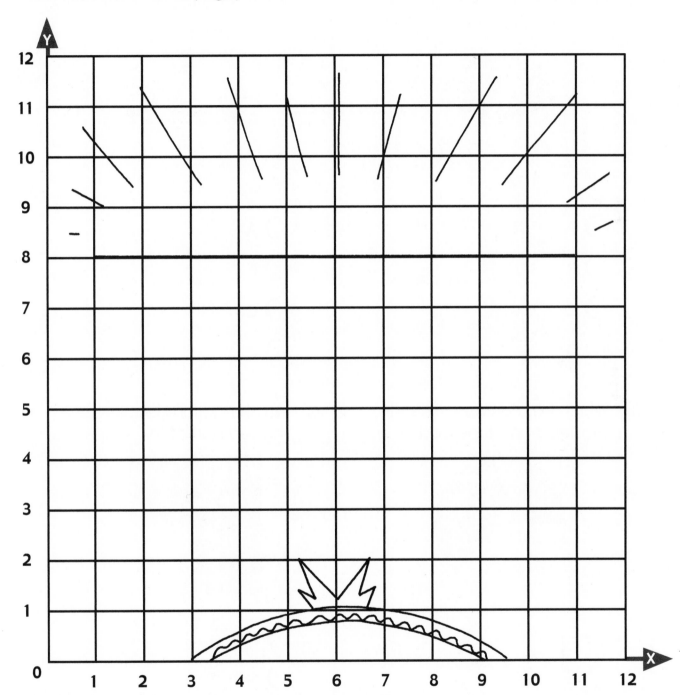

Answer: **a diamond**

Scholastic

Fractions & Graphs Practice Test

Fill in the bubble next to the correct answer.

1. Which fraction describes the shaded part of the circle?

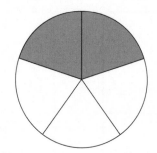

- ○ A $\frac{3}{5}$
- ○ B $\frac{2}{5}$
- ○ C $\frac{1}{3}$
- ○ D $\frac{1}{4}$

2. Which fraction describes the shaded part of the circle?

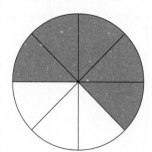

- ○ F $\frac{3}{4}$
- ○ G $\frac{6}{8}$
- ○ H $\frac{5}{8}$
- ○ J $\frac{1}{2}$

3. Which fraction describes the shaded part of the square?

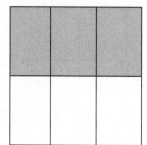

- ○ A $\frac{1}{6}$
- ○ B $\frac{2}{6}$
- ○ C $\frac{3}{6}$
- ○ D $\frac{4}{6}$

4. Which fraction describes the shaded part of the square?

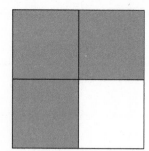

- ○ F $\frac{3}{4}$
- ○ G $\frac{2}{4}$
- ○ H $\frac{1}{4}$
- ○ J $\frac{1}{2}$

Scholastic

Fractions & Graphs Practice Test

Fill in the bubble next to the correct answer.

pizza	
hamburgers	
fries	
chicken fingers	
hot dogs	

Mrs. Jean's class took a survey to find out which foods the class liked best. Use the information on the bar graph to answer the questions.

5. Which was the class' favorite food?

- ◯ **A** hot dogs
- ◯ **B** pizza
- ◯ **C** fries
- ◯ **D** chicken fingers

6. Which food was the class' least favorite?

- ◯ **F** pizza
- ◯ **G** hot dogs
- ◯ **H** hamburgers
- ◯ **J** chicken fingers

7. Which food was the class' second favorite?

- ◯ **A** hot dogs
- ◯ **B** chicken fingers
- ◯ **C** pizza
- ◯ **D** fries

Scholastic

Fractions & Graphs Practice Test

Choose a sticker to place here.

Add the fractions and reduce the answer to the lowest common denominator.

Fill in the bubble next to the correct answer.

8. $\frac{3}{20} + \frac{2}{20} =$

- ○ A $\frac{1}{4}$
- ○ B $\frac{1}{5}$
- ○ C $\frac{2}{5}$
- ○ D $\frac{4}{10}$

10. $\frac{1}{5} + \frac{2}{5} =$

- ○ A $\frac{1}{2}$
- ○ B $\frac{1}{3}$
- ○ C $\frac{6}{10}$
- ○ D $\frac{3}{5}$

9. $\frac{2}{16} + \frac{2}{16} =$

- ○ F $\frac{1}{2}$
- ○ G $\frac{1}{3}$
- ○ H $\frac{1}{4}$
- ○ J $\frac{4}{16}$

11. $\frac{4}{8} + \frac{2}{8} =$

- ○ F $\frac{6}{8}$
- ○ G $\frac{1}{4}$
- ○ H $\frac{3}{4}$
- ○ J $\frac{2}{3}$

Scholastic

Geometric Shapes, Time & Money

How are a ball and the sun alike? What time is it? How much money will you earn mowing lawns today? This section prepares your child to answer questions like these. The answers may be important to what he or she does today or tomorrow.

What to Do

Have your child work out the problems on each activity page. Check the answers together. For a quick check, look at the answer key at the back of the book.

Keep On Going!

Play 20 questions. Make up questions concerning geometric shapes, time, and money for your child to answer. Have him or her make up questions for you to answer. Ask questions such as *It's 5:30, we'll have dinner in an hour, what time will it be then? If you have $10.00 and buy a movie ticket for $5.50 and a bag of popcorn for $2.50, how much money will you have left? What is the difference between a square and a cube?*

How many triangles and squares can you count in these geometric figures?

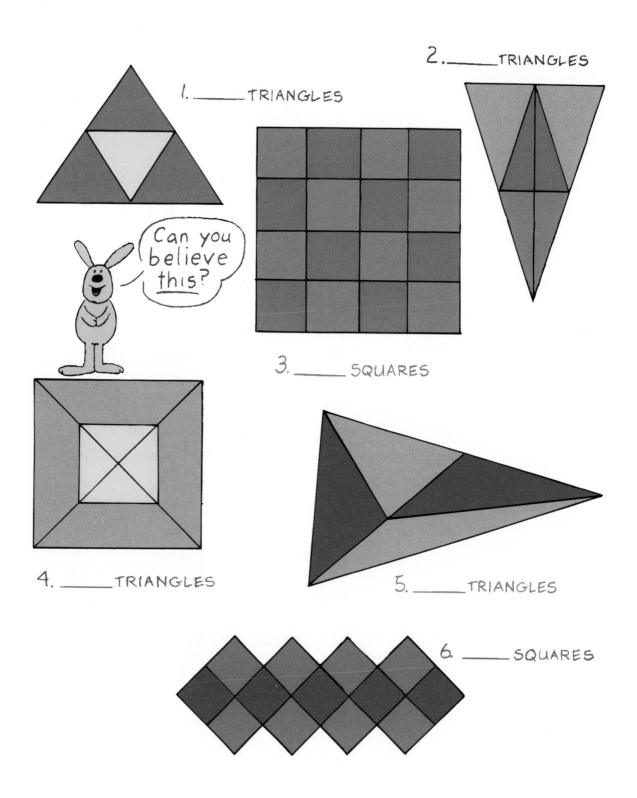

1. _____ TRIANGLES

2. _____ TRIANGLES

3. _____ SQUARES

4. _____ TRIANGLES

5. _____ TRIANGLES

6. _____ SQUARES

Can you believe this?

FLAT SHAPES HAVE LENGTH AND WIDTH.

A
SQUARE

B
CIRCLE

C
RECTANGLE

D
TRIANGLE

SOLID SHAPES HAVE LENGTH AND WIDTH AND DEPTH.

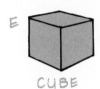
E
CUBE

F
SPHERE

G
CYLINDER

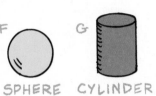
H
CONE

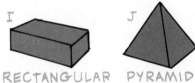
I
RECTANGULAR PRISM

J
PYRAMID

MATCH THE SHAPES WITH THESE OBJECTS. USE THE LETTERS ABOVE.

A.

1.	BALL
2.	WASTEBASKET
3.	RING
4.	POSTAGE STAMP
5.	BIRDHOUSE
6.	CRAYON BOX
7.	ICE CUBE
8.	APOLLO SPACECRAFT
9.	TRASH BARREL
10.	JAR
11.	ENVELOPE

B.

1.	COMPACT DISC
2.	AN ORANGE
3.	A PENNANT
4.	A BUILDING
5.	FISH BOWL
6.	CHILD'S BLOCK
7.	CHECKERS (GAME)
8.	A SAIL ON A SMALL BOAT
9.	CEREAL BOX
10.	PLANET EARTH
11	STICK OF BUTTER

C.

1.	ROAD MARKER
2.	FLAG
3.	SHEET OF PAPER
4.	FLASHLIGHT
5.	SOUP CAN
6.	POSTER
7.	BASEBALL
8.	TRAIN CAR
9.	A DIME
10.	PHOTOGRAPH
11.	WORLD GLOBE

Scholastic

Read the riddle. To find the answer, find the clock face that matches the time written under each blank line. Then write the letter under that clock face on the blank line.

Riddle: **What did the little hand on the clock say to the big hand?**

Answer. "___ ___ ___ ___ ___ ___ ___
       10:00   3:30   3:30   6:05   2:25   3:45   6:15

___ ___ ___ ___ ___ ___ !"
 4:45   6:05   2:55   3:45   3:45   2:55

O   U   E   N

T   Y   M   A

Scholastic

The big hand or *minute hand* on a clock tells you how many minutes it is past the hour.

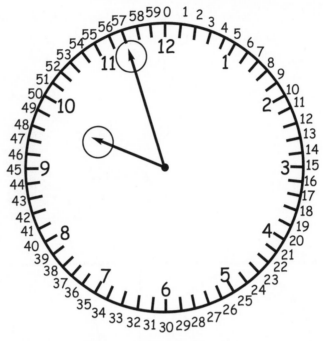

The small hand is pointing between the 9 and 10. The big hand or minute hand is pointing to the number 57. The time is 9:57.

Write the number that each minute hand is pointing to.
Write the time.

1.	**2.**	**3.**

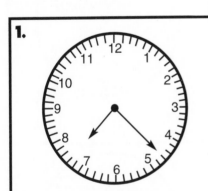

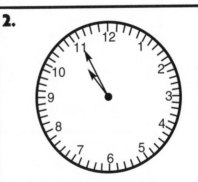

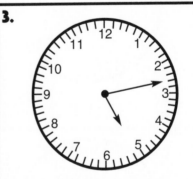

1. The minute hand is pointing to _____.

The time is

_____:_____

2. The minute hand is pointing to _____.

The time is

_____:_____

3. The minute hand is pointing to _____.

The time is

_____:_____

Scholastic

On each clock, draw where the minute hand should go.

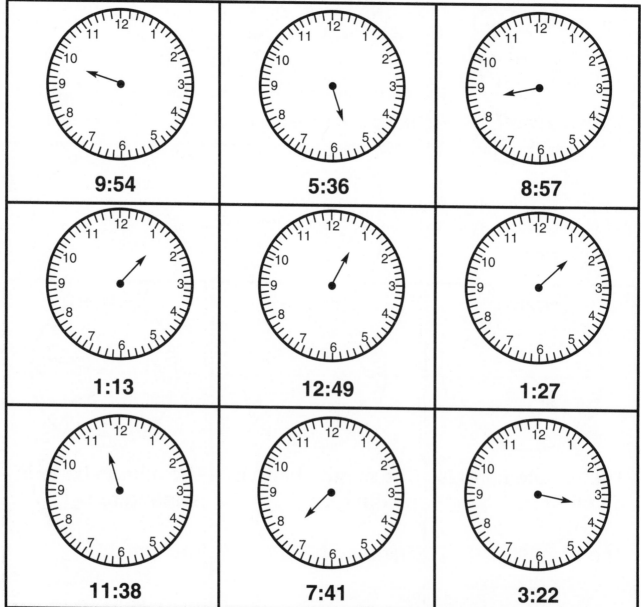

9:54	**5:36**	**8:57**
1:13	**12:49**	**1:27**
11:38	**7:41**	**3:22**

Scholastic

A. Count by fives to fill in the minutes for each number on the clock.

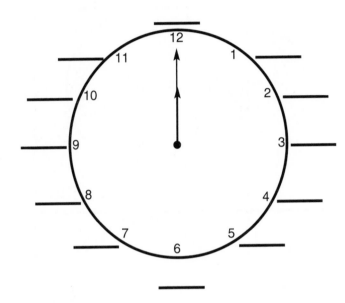

B. Fill in the blank with the time shown on each clock.

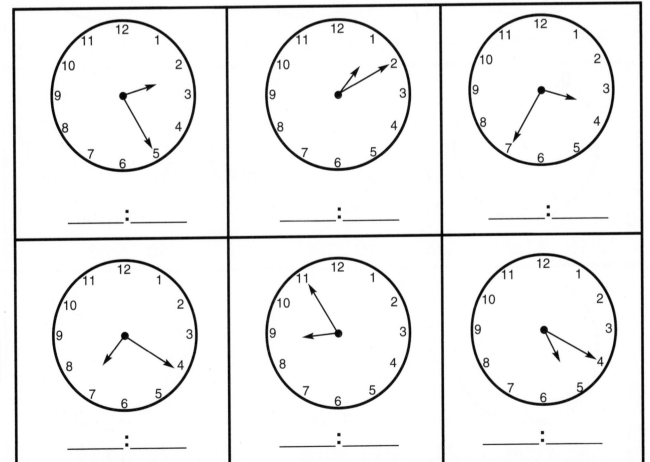

_____:_____

_____:_____

_____:_____

_____:_____

_____:_____

_____:_____

Scholastic

Draw a circle around the correct time underneath each clock.

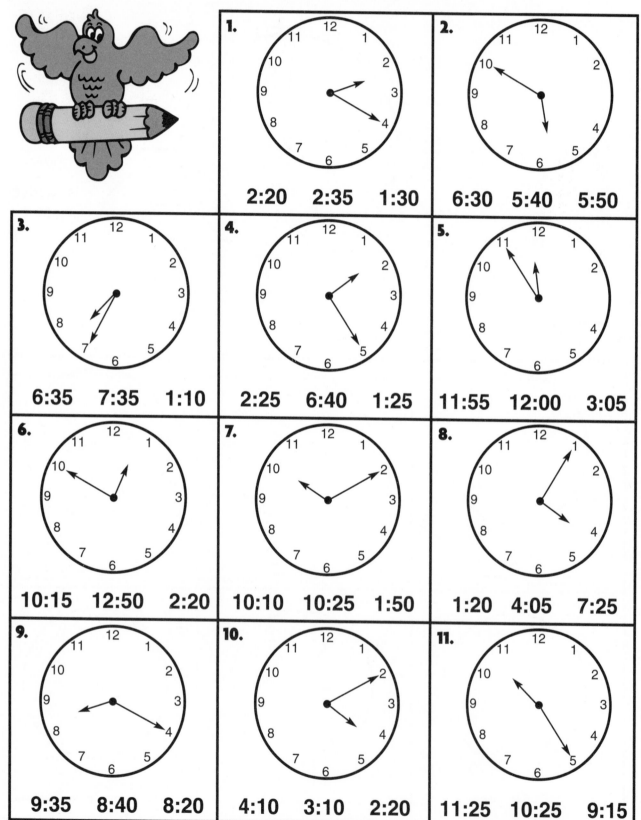

1.

2:20   2:35   1:30

2.

6:30   5:40   5:50

3.

6:35   7:35   1:10

4.

2:25   6:40   1:25

5.

11:55   12:00   3:05

6.

10:15   12:50   2:20

7.

10:10   10:25   1:50

8.

1:20   4:05   7:25

9.

9:35   8:40   8:20

10.

4:10   3:10   2:20

11.

11:25   10:25   9:15

Scholastic

You can write the time in words.

It is twelve
o'clock.

It is twelve
thirty.

It is twelve
fifteen.

It is twelve
forty-five.

Write the time shown on the clocks below in words.

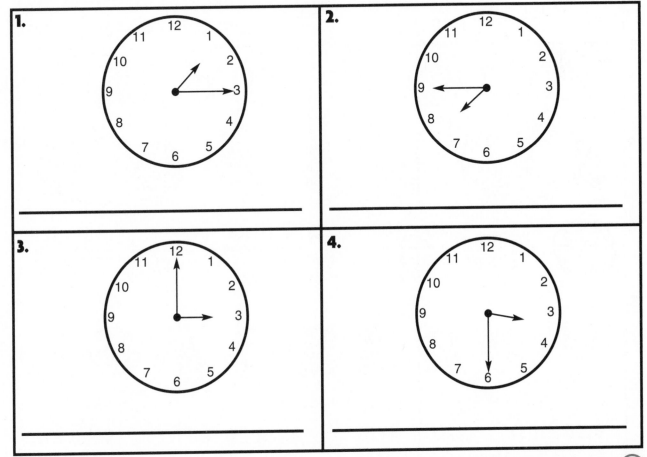

1.

_____

2.

_____

3.

_____

4.

_____

Scholastic

Circle the coins that you need to pay for each thing in the picture on page 271.

1. 🍎

2. Jelly

3. Cider

4. 🌽

5. 🎃

6. 🍐

7. 🥧

8. 🛒

Scholastic

Take a look at the signs on Bob's store. Circle any mistakes you see.
Then fix the mistakes so that the signs are correct.

BOB'S BIKE BARN

Bike
Helmets
$14.999

OPEN
9:30 AM - 8:75 PM

OPEN
8 DAYS
A WEEK

* SALE *
$10 off selected
Mountain Bikes
Were $139.99
Now $129.00

Handlebar Tape
$3.99 a roll
Buy two for $7.99
SAVE $1.00

Bicycle Baskets
$12.99 each
Two for $25.00
SAVE $.98

* FREE *
Bicycle
Stickers
$.10 each

Bicycle Chain
$.50 an inch
That's only $5.00 a foot

½ off all
Bicycle Seats
Were $17.00
Now $9.50

Scholastic

How many ways can you make a dollar? Write the number of coins you will need.

1.			
2.			
3.			
4.			
5.			
6.			
7.			
8.			
9.			
10.			
11.			
12.			
13.			
14.			
15.			

Write how many of each.

SHOW 63¢ FOUR WAYS.

16. _____ _____ _____

17. _____ _____ _____

18. _____ _____ _____

19. _____ _____ _____

Scholastic

Match the fronts and backs of the bills.

1.    **a.**

2.    **b.**

3.    **c.**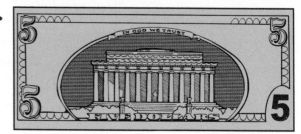

Fill in the blanks.

4. One dollar = _____ pennies.

5. One dollar = _____ nickels.

6. One dollar = _____ quarters.

7. Five dollars = _____ dimes.

8. Five dollars = _____ quarters.

9. Five dollars = _____ nickels.

10. Ten dollars = _____ quarters.

Scholastic

Find the value of each group of money.

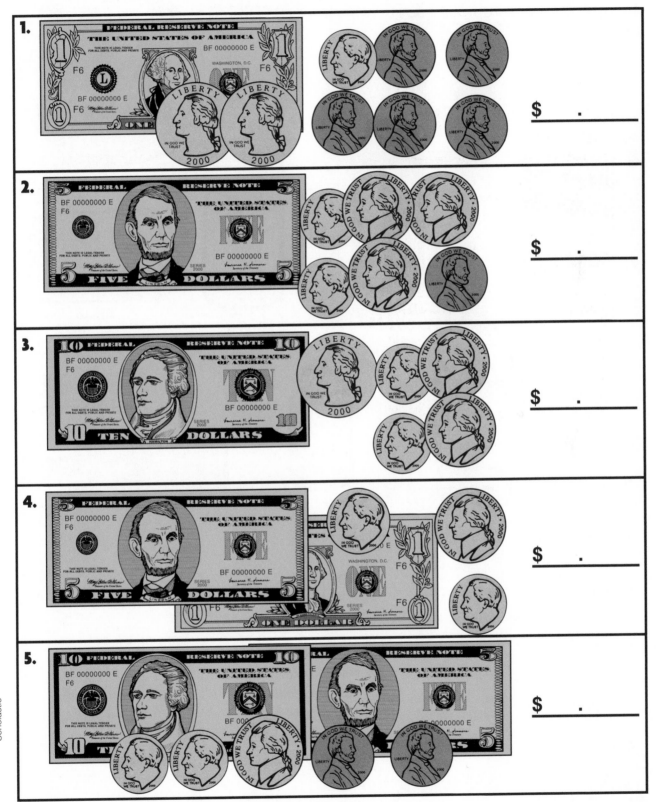

1. $ _____ . _____

2. $ _____ . _____

3. $ _____ . _____

4. $ _____ . _____

5. $ _____ . _____

Scholastic

Below are items found in a grocery and their cost. Read each person's shopping list and use mental math to figure out how much each person spent.

Cereal
$2.00

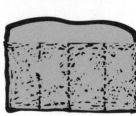

Milk
$1.25

Coffee
$3.00

Bread
$1.50

Soda
$1.50

Peanut butter
$1.50

Chewing gum
$.25

Toothpaste
$2.50

Ken's Shopping List

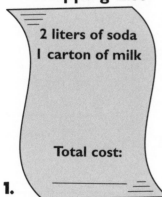

2 liters of soda
1 carton of milk

Total cost:

1. _____

Olivia's Shopping List

1 jar of peanut butter

1 box of cereal

1 can of coffee

1 loaf of bread

Total cost:

2. _____

Annette's Shopping List

1 jar of peanut butter

1 box of cereal

1 carton of milk

1 loaf of bread

Total cost:

3. _____

Scholastic

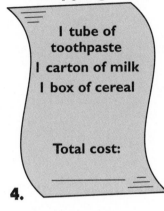

Bella's Shopping List

1 tube of toothpaste
1 carton of milk
1 box of cereal

Total cost:

_____

4.

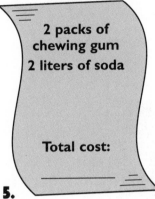

Todd's Shopping List

2 packs of chewing gum
2 liters of soda

Total cost:

_____

5.

Marianne's Shopping List

2 boxes of cereal
2 cartons of milk

Total cost:

_____

6.

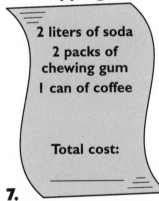

Ben's Shopping List

2 liters of soda
2 packs of chewing gum
1 can of coffee

Total cost:

_____

7.

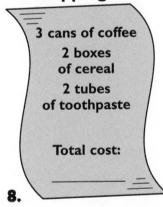

Brian's Shopping List

3 cans of coffee
2 boxes of cereal
2 tubes of toothpaste

Total cost:

_____

8.

Tucker's Shopping List

1 liter of soda
4 packs of chewing gum
1 jar of peanut butter

Total cost:

_____

9.

Write About It

10. Explain how you figured out how much Brian spent at the supermarket.

_____

_____

Scholastic

Geometric Shapes, Time & Money Practice Test

Fill in the bubble next to the correct answer.

1. Which of the following geometric shapes is flat?

○ **A** cylinder

○ **B** pyramid

○ **C** rectangle

○ **D** sphere

2. Which of the following shapes is solid?

○ **F** square

○ **G** sphere

○ **H** circle

○ **J** triangle

3. How many rectangles are in the pattern?

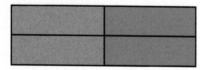

○ **A** 4

○ **B** 6

○ **C** 9

○ **D** 5

4. Which shape is a solid form of a triangle?

○ **F** cube

○ **G** sphere

○ **H** pyramid

○ **J** cylinder

Scholastic

Geometric Shapes, Time & Money Practice Test

Fill in the bubble next to the correct answer.

5. How much money would you need to buy 2 hot dogs, 3 pretzels, and 3 sodas?

- ○ **A** $6.33
- ○ **B** $6.75
- ○ **C** $5.95
- ○ **D** $6.03

6. How much money would you need to buy 4 bags of popcorn, 1 snow cone, and 1 cotton candy?

- ○ **F** $1.46
- ○ **G** $2.46
- ○ **H** $3.13
- ○ **J** $2.57

7. How much would 6 bags of popcorn cost?

- ○ **A** $1.13
- ○ **B** $.1.89
- ○ **C** $2.06
- ○ **D** $1.74

8. If you buy 3 hotdogs, and you give the vendor $5.00, how much money will you get back?

- ○ **F** $1.19
- ○ **G** $2.84
- ○ **H** $3.13
- ○ **J** $2.96

Scholastic

Geometric Shapes, Time & Money Practice Test

Choose a sticker to place here.

Fill in the bubble next to the correct answer.

9. If you leave your house at 9:00 in the morning and you travel for an hour and a half. What time is it?

- ○ **A** 9:30
- ○ **B** 10:00
- ○ **C** 10:30
- ○ **D** 11:00

10. You leave the game at 4:00. It snowed so hard it took 5 hours to get home. What time was it when you reached home?

- ○ **F** 7:00
- ○ **G** 8:00
- ○ **H** 9:00
- ○ **J** 10:00

11. It is 8:00. You are expecting a package at 11:45. How long will you have to wait?

- ○ **A** 3 hours and 15 minutes
- ○ **B** 2 hours and 45 minutes
- ○ **C** 3 hours and 45 minutes
- ○ **D** 1 hour and 45 minutes

12. It is 5:00 in your city. Your sister lives in a city that is 2 hours earlier. What time is it in her city?

- ○ **F** 4:00
- ○ **G** 3:00
- ○ **H** 2:00
- ○ **J** 7:00

Scholastic

Get Ready for
Grade 4

In this section of the workbook, your child will get a preview of the skills he or she will learn and expand upon in Grade 4. The activity pages in this section were chosen to help your child develop the skills necessary to be successful. Here are some of the skills and concepts covered:

• Identifying unusual vowel sounds and their spellings

• Identifying and using prefixes and suffixes

• Identifying and using analogies, onomatopoeic words, and oxymorons

• Identifying and using words from other languages

• Using reading comprehension skills

• Combining sentences

• Identifying and using conjunctions and prepositions

• Identifying and using similes and metaphors

• Understanding basic concepts related to addition, subtraction, multiplication, and division of whole numbers and fractions

• Using mathematical strategies to solve word problems

The **/ou/ sound** *can be spelled with the letters* ow *or* ou.
The **/oi/ sound** *can be spelled with the letters* oi *or* oy.

A **noun** *is a word that names a person, place, or thing.*
A **verb** *is a word that shows an action.*

Read and write each word. Look for the word that can be both a noun and a verb. Then organize the list words as nouns or verbs.

List Words	nouns	verbs
1. moisture	_____	_____
2. destroy	_____	_____
3. allow	_____	_____
4. council	_____	_____
5. avoid	_____	_____
6. employ	_____	_____
7. boundary	_____	_____
8. downtown	_____	
9. boiled	_____	
10. voyage	_____	
11. mountain	_____	
12. disappoint	_____	
13. allowance	_____	
14. found	_____	
15. oyster	_____	

both noun and verb

_____

Challenge Words

16. exercise _____

17. heartbeat _____

18. muscle _____

19. oxygen _____

20. breathe _____

Scholastic

Complete each analogy with a list word.

1. *Studied* is to *observed* as _____ is to *discovered.*

2. *Lake* is to *ocean* as *hill* is to _____.

3. *Seed* is to *apple* as *pearl* is to _____.

4. *Laugh* is to *comedian* as _____ is to *enemy.*

5. *Cookie* is to *snack* as *money* is to _____.

6. *Heal* is to *doctor* as _____ is to *boss.*

Write the missing vowels for each word.

7. v__y__ g__

8. c__ __ nc__l

9. b__ __l__d

10. __l l__w

11. m__ __st__r__

12. b__ __nd__ry

13. d__s__pp__ __nt

14. d__wnt__wn

15. d__str__y

Circle each challenge word on the track. Then write the remaining letters on the blanks below to learn an interesting fact about exercising.

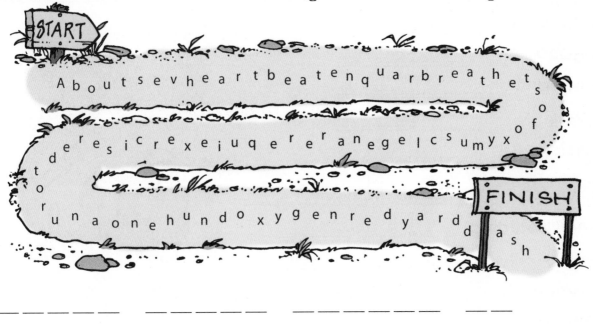

_ _ _ _ _   _ _ _ _ _ _ _ _   _ _ _ _ _ _   _ _ _ _ _

_ _ _ _ _ _ _   _ _ _ _ _   _ _ _ _ _ _ _ _   _ _

_ _ _   _ _ _ _ _ _ - _ _ _ _ _ _ _   _ _ _ _ .

Scholastic

The /k/ **sound** *can be spelled with the letters* c, k, or ck.

Read and write each word. Then organize the list words alphabetically using the guide words.

 List Words

atomic/freckle

1. nickel _____ _____ _____

2. tractor _____ _____ _____

3. picnic _____ _____

4. cracker _____

5. clerk _____

handicap/picture

6. heroic _____ _____

7. hockey _____ _____ _____

8. rocket _____ _____

9. shriek _____

10. attic _____

pink/trademark

11. frantic _____ _____ _____

12. attack _____ _____ _____

13. hawk _____ _____

14. plastic _____

15. stack _____

Challenge Words

16. Olympic _____

17. snowboarding _____

18. skiing _____

19. competition _____

20. athletes _____

Scholastic

A. Look at the shape of the list words. Write the word that fits in each set of letter boxes.

1.

2.

3.

4.

5.

6.

7.

Unscramble each group of letters to write two list words.

8. ckerelkccrar   _____   _____

9. croikehtocre   _____   _____

10. tanpcricnifci   _____   _____

11. skrcatortcat   _____   _____

B. Complete the passage using the challenge words. Then use the number code to learn about an exciting winter sport.

The first Winter ___ ___ ___ ___ ___ ___ ___ Games were held in 1924.
⠀⠀⠀⠀⠀⠀⠀⠀⠀⠀⠀⠀⠀⠀4

The ___ ___ ___ ___ ___ ___ ___ ___ ___ featured skating and
⠀⠀⠀⠀⠀3⠀⠀⠀⠀⠀⠀6

___ ___ ___ ___ ___ ___. In 1998, ___ ___ ___ ___ ___ ___ ___ ___ ___ ___ ___
⠀2⠀⠀⠀8⠀⠀⠀⠀⠀⠀⠀⠀⠀⠀1⠀⠀⠀⠀⠀⠀⠀⠀7

became an Olympic sport. ___ ___ ___ ___ ___ ___ ___ from about 80
⠀⠀⠀⠀⠀⠀⠀⠀⠀⠀⠀⠀⠀⠀⠀⠀⠀⠀⠀5

countries competed in the 2002 Winter Olympic Games.

Athletes sled headfirst at speeds over 80 miles per hour in the

___ ___ ___ ___ ___ ___ ___ ___ event!
⠀1⠀2⠀3⠀4⠀5⠀6⠀7⠀8

A **prefix** is a word part that is added to the beginning of a word and changes its meaning. Here are some common prefixes and their meanings.

a-	on	**mis-**	wrong	**re-**	again, back
anti-	against	**multi-**	many, much	**super-**	above, beyond
im-	not	**non-**	not	**trans-**	across
in-	not	**over-**	too much	**un-**	not
inter-	among, between	**pre-**	before	**under-**	below, less than

Here are some words with these prefixes. Use the information from the chart above to write what you think each word means. Then use a dictionary to check your definitions. Make corrections if needed.

1. **aboard** _____

2. **supervisor** _____

3. **multicolored** _____

4. **misunderstood** _____

5. **international** _____

6. **preheat** _____

7. **nonstop** _____

8. **transcontinental** _____

9. **uncomfortable** _____

10. **overpriced** _____

11. **review** _____

12. **unbelievable** _____

13. **inexpensive** _____

14. **underweight** _____

15. **impatient** _____

16. **antifreeze** _____

TRANSCONTINENTAL EXPRESS • GATE 2

ALL ABOARD!

Scholastic

*The prefix **dis-** can mean "not" or "opposite of." Draw a line between the prefix and base word in the chart below. Think about how the meaning of the base word changes when **dis-** is added.*

discontinued	disagree	dislike
discover	dishonest	disconnect
disobey	disappear	disapprove

Now use the words to complete the sentences.

1. Activities at the recreation center have been _____ until further notice.

2. You can _____ the electric clock by pulling out the plug.

3. Instead of studying, the _____ student cheated by copying the test answers from another student.

4. My brother always seems to _____ from sight whenever there is work to be done around the house.

5. If you would at least taste the soup, you might _____ that it is really quite good.

6. My parents sometimes _____ with me about which CDs to buy because they _____ of the content.

7. I really _____ doing homework as soon as I get home from school and would rather do something fun.

8. What is the punishment if you _____ the rules?

A **suffix** is a group of letters that are added to the end of a word and can add meaning to it. Some common suffixes and their meanings are listed in the box below.

-ous	full of	**-ward**	direction
-less	without	**-ity**	condition of
-ment	action or process	**-en**	to make
-ent	one who	**-ology**	science or study of
-an	relating to	**-ily**	in what manner

One state grows enough apples each year to circle the Earth at least 25 times. Do you know which state this is? To find out, use the suffixes to write a word for each definition. The letters in the boxes will answer the question.

1. in the direction of the east __ __ __ __ ☐ __ __ __

2. in a hearty manner __ __ ☐ __ __ __ __ __

3. one who resides in a place __ __ ☐ __ __ __ __ __

4. full of treachery __ __ __ __ __ ☐ __ __

5. relating to America __ __ __ __ ☐ __ __

6. the act of governing __ __ __ __ __ ☐ __ __ __ __

7. the study of animals __ __ __ __ __ ☐ __

8. Something that is necessary __ __ __ __ __ __ __ ☐ __

9. without noise __ ☐ __ __ __ __ __ __

10. to make weak __ __ __ __ __ ☐

11. Name of state _____

Scholastic

An **analogy** *is a comparison of two sets of similar objects or things.*

Think about how the first pair of words is related. Then write the word that completes the second part of the analogy. Use the words in the box or another word you know that fits.

conductor	cashier	custodian
astronaut	professor	paratrooper
geologist	architect	archaeologist
hairdresser	physician	astronomer

1. *Spade* is to *gardener* as *baton* is to _____.

2. *Athlete* is to *team* as _____ is to *faculty*.

3. *Lawyer* is to *courtroom* as _____ is to *salon*.

4. *Pattern* is to *seamstress* as *blueprint* is to _____.

5. *Cook* is to *chef* as *clean* is to _____.

6. *Scuba* is to *diver* as *parachute* is to _____.

7. *Mechanic* is to *garage* as _____ is to *space station*.

8. *Screwdriver* is to *carpenter* as *stethoscope* is to _____.

9. *Books* are to *librarian* as *rocks* are to _____.

10. *Flight attendant* is to *airplane* as _____ is to *supermarket*.

11. *Collector* is to *taxes* as _____ is to *artifacts*.

12. *Lasso* is to *cowhand* as *telescope* is to _____.

Scholastic

Buzz, hiss, fizz, and hoot *imitate sounds. They are called* **onomatopoeic** *words. Here are more words. Think about their sounds as you say each one aloud. Then list other words you know that imitate sounds.*

sniffle	swish	rumble	crunch	whish	slurp
sizzle	crackle	clatter	hiccup	thud	screech
whir	zing	sputter	clomp	burp	splash
_____	_____	_____	_____	_____	_____
_____	_____	_____	_____	_____	_____

A. Complete each sentence with a word from the box. Add *-ed* to the word when necessary.

1. It is not polite to _____ your soup.

2. As the storm approached, we could hear the _____ of thunder.

3. The steaks began to _____ on the grill.

4. The packed snow _____ under our feet.

5. The book fell from the shelf and hit the floor with a _____.

6. If you drink that soda pop too fast, you are sure to _____.

7. The burning logs _____ in the fireplace.

8. The child _____ across the floor in his father's boots.

9. The _____ of the owl startled me the first time I heard it.

10. As soon as I flipped the switch, the motor began to _____.

B. Now write original sentences using onomatopoeic words you listed.

1. _____

2. _____

3. _____

4. _____

5. _____

6. _____

Scholastic

Accidentally on purpose *is a called an* **oxymoron** *because words that make up the phrase contradict each other.*

Create an oxymoron by writing a word from the box next to the underlined word in each sentence.

random	inside
original	bitter
estimate	minor
whisper	sorrow
awfully	unfinished
serious	ugly
shrimp	half
misunderstood	

1. Mason ordered a plate of <u>jumbo</u> _____.

2. I bought a desk that was <u>completely</u> _____.

3. Meg sliced the sandwich and gave me the <u>larger</u> _____.

4. We made cookies with _____ <u>sweet</u> chocolate chips.

5. It is time for some _____ <u>fun</u>!

6. That shirt is <u>pretty</u> _____.

7. I <u>clearly</u> _____ what you were trying to say.

8. Who said that parting is <u>sweet</u> _____?

9. Speaking in a <u>loud</u> _____, we heard what he did not want us to hear.

10. My day was one _____ <u>disaster</u> after another.

11. Did you know that your shirt is _____ <u>out</u>?

12. I have an _____ <u>copy</u> of the letter.

13. Please make an <u>exact</u> _____ of what you will need.

14. The children arranged themselves in _____ <u>order</u>.

15. The soup tasted _____ <u>good</u>.

Scholastic

Many words in the English language have been adopted from other languages.

Chinese	Dutch	Russian	Hindi	Spanish	German
Arabic	Turkish	Japanese	Yiddish	Italian	French

What language do you think each of the following words comes from? Write your guess. Then use a dictionary to check. The dictionary entry for *mammoth* tells that it comes from the Russian language.

mammoth \\'ma-məth\ *n* a large, extinct elephant that had long curved tusks and was covered with hair. (1706) [Russian *mamont, mamot*]

	Guess	Check
1. delicatessen	_____	_____
2. shampoo	_____	_____
3. chow	_____	_____
4. pickle	_____	_____
5. bouquet	_____	_____
6. macaroni	_____	_____
7. borscht	_____	_____
8. judo	_____	_____
9. coyote	_____	_____
10. sherbet	_____	_____
11. pastrami	_____	_____
12 alfalfa	_____	_____
13. pumpernickel	_____	_____
14. bologna	_____	_____
15. potato	_____	_____
16. detour	_____	_____

Sequencing *is when events are arranged in the order in which they happened.*

Many linking words help a writer to move through the sequencing more smoothly. Words like *now, then, when, soon, next, later, while, before,* and *after* tie the sentences together.

A. There are sequencing words used in each sentence below. Underline the sequencing words in each sentence.

1. Before we went to the party, we wrapped our gifts.
2. Everyone jumped into the van, and then drove to Joe's house.
3. When we arrived, we saw all the beautiful decorations.
4. After greeting our host, we put our gifts on the table.
5. Soon other guests began to arrive.
6. Next, Joe thanked his friends for coming over.
7. While Joe opened his gifts, the guests were served cake and soda.
8. After, a comic told jokes.
9. Finally, it was time to leave.
10. Now, we can just go home.

then	next	after	at last	first

B. Choose words from the word bank above to fill in the blanks.

Colleen was thrilled; **1.**_____ the day of the big volleyball match was here! **2.**_____ a brief morning practice, the team ate breakfast together and the coach sent them home to rest. Colleen took a short nap and called a teammate to discuss strategy. **3.**_____ it was time to return to the gym. **4.**_____Colleen put on her kneepads, **5.**_____ she put on her elbow pads. She was ready to go!

The **main idea** *tells what a story or paragraph is mostly about.*

Read the letters Tyler wrote from camp and those he received. Write the main idea for each letter.

Dear Mom and Dad,   Saturday, June 7

Camp is great! I have met a lot of new friends. Jimmy is from California, Eric is from Iowa, and Tony is from Missouri. We have a great time together, swimming, canoeing, hiking, and playing tricks on other campers! Every night, we sneak over to another cabin. We then try to scare the other campers either by making scary noises or by throwing things at their cabin. It's so funny to see them run out screaming! Now don't worry, Mom. I'm not going to get caught like I did last year.

One thing that is different from last year is how many bugs there are! I know that scientists discover 7 to 10 thousand new kinds of insects each year, and I think they could discover even more here! I have at least 100 itchy mosquito bites and about 20 fire ant bites. Every time I go outside, horseflies chase me, too! Other than all these buggy bugs, I'm having the best time!

Love,
Tyler

Main idea _____

Dear Tyler,   Tuesday, June 10

Are you sure you are okay? All of those bugs sound awful! Have you used all of the "Itch-Be-Gone" cream I got you? You know how your feet swell if you don't use the cream! How about the "Ants 'R Awful" lotion for the ant bites? You and your Aunt Ethel have always seemed to attract those nasty fire ants.

Now Tyler, I am very happy that you have met some new friends and that you are having fun together. However, you MUST stop trying to scare other campers. Remember, honey, some campers may frighten easily. I want you to apologize for any anxiety you may have caused them and start being the nice, polite boy that I know you are. Do you hear me, Tyler? Please be careful. I want you home safely.

Love,
Mom

Scholastic

Main idea _____

Dear Steven,   Saturday, June 7

Camp is amazing this year! Our guides help us do the coolest stuff. Like yesterday, we hiked for six miles until we found this awesome spring. Then we used a rope hanging on a tree to jump in the water. I went so high that I made a huge splash! Thursday, our guides took us rowing. We rowed to this little island where we made a bonfire. We roasted the fish we had caught. My fish was the biggest, of course!

Last night, we collected a big bunch of frogs in a bag. Then we put the bag under a bed in another cabin while they were all at the campfire. When they got back, the frogs were all over their cabin. We laughed so hard! I know they're going get us back. I've seen them planning. I can't wait to see what they try. Hey! How's the leg? Sure wish you were here!

Your friend,
Tyler

Main idea _____

Dear Tyler,   Tuesday, June 10

That's great you're having so much fun! I wish I were there. All I do is sit around bumming out, thinking about all the fun you are having. I can't believe I broke my leg two days before camp started. My mom keeps renting me movies and video games, but I think I've seen everything and played everything. I just know I won't be happy again until this cast is off.

Your new friends sound great! Sure wish I was there helping you guys play tricks on the other campers. Remember last year when we smeared honey all over another cabin and all those bees came? That was so funny—except the part where we had to scrub all the cabins clean wearing hot, protective gear. I'm still surprised they let you come back this summer!

Hey! What's up with all the bugs? Your mom called my mom all worried about a bunch of bugs or something. Have fun and write soon!

Your friend,
Steven

Main idea _____

Scholastic

*To better understand a character, a reader needs to carefully study, or **analyze**, a character's traits, personality, motivations, relationships, and strengths and weaknesses.*

One day, Lindsay and Erica were sitting at Lindsay's house working very diligently. Fourth grade was tough, and they were working on a science project about weather. Lindsay was a hard worker like Erica, so the two girls were happy to have each other as partners. They were currently writing about rain and were amazed to learn how much rain Hawaii gets. Lindsay found that Mount Waialeale, on the island of Kauai, gets about 420 inches of rain a year! In 1982, Mount Waialeale set a world record when it received 666 inches of rain. The girls knew that their classmates would find all these facts interesting.

The girls were enjoying the fun facts they were finding when all of a sudden, Lindsay saw Erica choking. Erica had been chewing on a pen cap and had accidentally swallowed it! Erica started pointing to her neck. Lindsay asked her if she was choking. When Erica nodded to say yes, Lindsay quickly got her mom to do the Heimlich maneuver to try to help Erica stop choking. (The Heimlich maneuver is a way to save someone from choking. This method is named after the doctor who invented it, Henry Heimlich.)

Lindsay's mom did not want to hurt Erica, so the first time she tried the Heimlich maneuver, she did not do it very hard. She tried a second time, and nothing happened. After trying it a third time, the pen cap flew out of Erica's mouth!

Erica was very grateful to Lindsay and her mom. She had been terrified when she realized she had swallowed the pen cap and could not breathe. Lindsay's quick thinking saved her friend. This was one science project that both girls would never forget!

Scholastic

1. Circle each word that describes Lindsay.

   hard worker   boring   brave   fast-thinking

   quick-acting   selfish   timid   lazy

2. Circle each word that tells how Erica might have been feeling when she realized she was choking.

   scared   thankful   enthusiastic   helpless

   courageous   sick   alarmed   friendly

3. What do you think Lindsay might be when she grows up? _____

   _____

4. Write *L* for Lindsay, *E* for Erica, or *B* for both.

   ____ good students   ____ frightened   ____ persistent

   ____ dependable   ____ grateful   ____ appreciative

5. What is the name of the doctor who invented the lifesaving maneuver?

   _____

6. What place gets about 420 inches of rain a year? _____

7. Circle the average amount of rain Mount Waialeale received each day in 1982.

   almost 3"   just under 2"   just over 4"   about 1"

8. Why do you think this project will be one neither girl will ever forget?

   _____

   _____

   _____

Scholastic

Where Did We Get That Word?

The dancer put a cardigan sweater over her leotard. Then she sat down to eat a sandwich. *Cardigan, leotard, sandwich*—where did these words come from? Did you know that each of them was a person's name? Words that come from proper names are called *eponyms*, and there are many eponyms in English.

The sandwich, for example, was named for John Montagu, the Earl of Sandwich. He lived from 1718–1792. He loved to play cards and did not want to stop a game even to eat. By putting cold meat between two pieces of bread, he could eat while he played.

The cardigan sweater was named for an officer in the British army. In the 1800s, James Thomas Brudenell, the Earl of Cardigan, spent his own money to buy special knitted jackets for the men in his regiment. Knitted jackets with buttons soon came to be called *cardigans*.

Jules Leotard was a French circus performer. In 1859, at the age of twenty-one, Leotard performed the first mid-air somersault. He became known as the "daring young man on the flying trapeze." Leotard invented a close-fitting one-piece suit to wear when he performed. Dancers and acrobats still call their close-fitting garments *leotards*.

Another person who gave her name to a style of clothing was Amelia Bloomer. Bloomer was the editor of a magazine called *The Lily*. American women in her day were expected to wear heavy skirts that dragged on the floor. In 1851, a young woman named Elizabeth Smith Miller introduced a new kind of clothing that was much easier to move around in. She wore a dress that came only to the knees. Under it she wore baggy pants that fitted close at the ankles. Amelia Bloomer published a picture of the outfit in *The Lily*. She hoped women would adopt the new style. In news stories, reporters called the pants "bloomers." A hundred years later, people were still using the word *bloomers* for pants worn under a dress.

Scholastic

There are many other words that come from people's names. The *diesel* engine was named for its inventor, Rudolf Diesel. The word *boycott* comes from the name of an English landlord named Charles Boycott. Where each word came from is a story in itself. Who knows, maybe your name will become a word some day.

1. Which of these word stories would best fit in this article?

    Ⓐ *Armadillo* comes from a Spanish word meaning "armed." The animal's hard shell looks like armor.

    Ⓑ *Braille* is a system of writing for the blind that was developed by Louis Braille.

    Ⓒ *Cricket* is a word that imitates the sound a cricket makes.

    Ⓓ *Dynamite* comes from a Greek word meaning "power." Alfred Nobel, the inventor of dynamite, created the word.

2. Which of these words came from a person's name?

    Ⓕ trapeze

    Ⓖ editor

    Ⓗ boycott

    Ⓙ acrobat

3. What is this article mainly about?

    _____

    _____

4. Why did the Earl of Sandwich invent the "sandwich"?

    _____

    _____

5. What are "bloomers," and where did the word bloomers come from?

    _____

    _____

    _____

Scholastic

Prepositions *show the relationship between a noun or pronoun and another word or group of words in a sentence such as* **in, on, of, for,** *or* **at.** *Groups of words introduced by a preposition are called* **prepositional phrases.**

A. Read each sentence. Underline each group of words that begins with a preposition, and circle the preposition. Some sentences have more than one prepositional phrase.

1. The boy cut out pictures of mountains, rivers, and lakes.

2. He enjoyed pasting them on the walls of his room.

3. His father responded to the scenes in the pictures.

4. He decided that he would take his son on a camping trip.

5. They carried supplies in a backpack and knapsack.

6. The boy drank a hot drink from his father's mug.

7. That afternoon they hiked in the mountains for hours.

8. They were disappointed when they found many campers at the Lost Lake.

9. The boy and his father continued on their journey.

10. Finally, they stopped at a quiet place for the night.

11. The boy and his father ate and slept in a tent.

12. The tent kept them safe from the wind and rain.

13. Will this trip make the boy feel closer to his father?

14. What else will they see on their camping trip?

B. Complete each sentence with a prepositional phrase.

1. Let's go to the store

2. I just received a letter

3. Eduardo found his missing sneaker

4. Tanya always plays soccer

Scholastic

If two sentences share the same subject, information about the subject can be written as a phrase after the subject in the new sentence. Be sure to use commas to set apart the phrase from the rest of the sentence.

Sentence 1: **The Gateway Arch is America's tallest human-made monument.**

Sentence 2: **The monument rises 630 feet above the ground.**

Combined: **The Gateway Arch, America's tallest human-made monument, rises 630 feet above the ground.**

Read the sentences. Combine the ideas in each pair into one sentence by including information in a phrase after the subject in the sentence.

1. The Caspian Sea is the world's largest lake.
The lake covers an area about the same size as Montana.

_____

2. The Komodo dragon is a member of the monitor family.
It can grow to a length of 10 feet.

_____

3. Our closest star is the sun.
It is estimated to be more than 27,000,000°F.

_____

4. Ronald W. Reagan was our nation's 40th president.
He worked as a Hollywood actor for almost 30 years.

_____

5. Georgia is the state that grows the most peanuts.
It harvests over 2 billion pounds each year.

_____

6. Jackie Robinson was the first African American to play in the major leagues. He played for the Brooklyn Dodgers.

_____

Scholastic

Using the conjunction and, shows you are joining ideas of the same kind.
Using the conjunction but, shows the difference between two clauses.
Using the conjunction or, is usually showing a choice.

Write the correct conjunction in the blank.

1. Shelly loves seashells, _____ her collection is of coins.

2. Mama went on strike, _____ she quit cleaning up after us.

3. Mrs. Goodwin gave us a choice of behaving, _____ losing our recess.

4. Apple, oranges, _____ grapes are on the table for a snack.

5. I cannot decide if I want to go to summer camp, _____ to go stay with my best friend.

6. I know I have been well behaved, _____ I wonder if Santa saw me when I was acting up?

7. Sponge Bob is square, _____ he absorbs everything.

8. Mary loves summer vacation, _____ she is always ready to get back to school.

9. Jada can eat a big lunch, _____ she can wait and eat a big dinner.

10. Fred wants to be in the band and play tennis after school, _____ he cannot do both.

11. I like both Ted _____ Jim the same.

12. Did you want chicken _____ fish for dinner?

13. I thought she said "three," _____ she really said "tree."

14. Polly wants to go, _____ I want to stay.

Scholastic

You can compare two things that are not alike in order to give your readers a clearer and more colorful picture. When you use like *or as to make a comparison, it is called a* **simile**.

Max is as slow as molasses when he doesn't want to do something.
My sister leaped over the puddles like a frog to avoid getting her shoes wet.
The angry man erupted like a volcano.

When you make a comparison without like *or as, it is called a* **metaphor**. *You compare things directly, saying the subject is something else.*

The disturbed anthill was a whirlwind of activity.
The oak trees, silent sentries around the cabin, stood guard.
Jenny and I were all ears as we listened to the latest gossip.

Finish the metaphors and similes.

1. Crowds of commuters piled into the subway cars like _____

_____

2. Chirping crickets on warm summer night are_____

_____

3. After rolling in the mud, our dog looked like _____

4. Happiness is _____

5. Just learning to walk, the toddler was as wobbly as _____

_____

6. After scoring the winning point, I felt as_____

_____

7. Having a tooth filled is about as much fun as_____

_____

8. A summer thunderstorm is_____

_____

9. _____ is _____

10. _____ is like _____

Scholastic

Add the numbers.

1. 3,827
   + 903

2. 1,562
   + 843

3. 2,148
   + 674

4. 7,291
   + 629

5. 4,023
   + 721

6. 5,484
   + 648

7. 1,326
   + 984

8. 6,423
   + 422

9. 1,846
   + 221

10. 9,016
    + 112

11. 4,536
    + 119

12. 2,349
    + 824

13. 8,461
    + 714

14. 3,654
    + 582

15. 1,672
    + 432

16. 5,184
    + 686

17. 1,592
    + 768

18. 4,394
    + 184

19. 7,143
    + 527

20. 1,489
    + 368

Scholastic

Some addition problems will require regrouping several times. The steps look like this.

1. Add the ones column. Regroup if needed.

2. Add the tens column. Regroup if needed.

3. Add the hundreds column. Regroup if needed.

4. Continue working through each column in order.

1	11	111	111
37,462	37,462	37,462	37,462
+ 22,798	+ 22,798	+ 22,798	+ 22,798
0	60	260	60,260

Add. Then use the code to finish the fun fact below.

1.

bald eagle

Z.   953 + 418

B.   295 + 337

R.   418 + 793

Q.   565 + 957

S.   862 + 339

X.   478 + 283

2.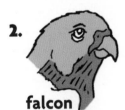

falcon

I.   2,428 + 6,679

C.   1,566 + 2,487

Y.   3,737 + 6,418

A.   9,289 + 4,735

Y.   8,754 + 368

3.

vulture

L.   57,854 + 45,614

P.   29,484 + 46,592

E.   36,238 + 46,135

F.   67,139 + 25,089

4.

owl

D.   240,669 + 298,727

O.   476,381 + 175,570

R.   882,948 + 176,524

What do all of these birds have in common?

They are _____ _____ _____ _____ _____   _____ _____

632   9,107   1,211   539,396   1,201   651,951   92,228

_____ _____ _____ _____ .

76,076   1,059,472   82,373   10,155

Scholastic

To multiply with zeros, follow these steps.

```
  9 0   9 x 2 = 18
x   2   Add a zero in
        the ones place
        to make 180.
```

```
  9 0   9 x 2 = 18
x 2 0   Add 2 zeros—one
        in the ones place
        and one in the
        tens place.
```

```
9 0 0   9 x 2 = 18
x 2 0   Add 3 zeros—one
        in the ones place,
        one in the tens
        place, and one in
        the hundreds
        place.
```

Multiply.

A.

```
    80        60        900        40        120        200
x    7    x   50    x    30    x    11    x     2    x    60
```

B.

```
    70       120         60       700         50         30
x    7    x  300    x    90    x    60    x    70    x    12
```

C.

```
   600        40         30         90        200         50
x   80    x    12    x     8    x    50    x   120    x     8
```

Scholastic

To multiply with a 2-digit factor that requires regrouping, follow these steps.

1. Multiply by the ones digit.

$$
\begin{array}{r}
3 \\
46 \\
\times \quad 26 \\
\hline
276
\end{array}
$$

2. Place a zero in the ones column..

$$
\begin{array}{r}
3 \\
46 \\
\times \quad 26 \\
\hline
276 \\
0
\end{array}
$$

3. Multiply by the tens digit.

$$
\begin{array}{r}
3 \\
46 \\
\times \quad 26 \\
\hline
276 \\
+\ 920
\end{array}
$$

4. Add to find the product.

$$
\begin{array}{r}
1 \\
3 \\
46 \\
\times \quad 26 \\
\hline
276 \\
+\ 920 \\
\hline
1,196
\end{array}
$$

Multiply. Then use the code to answer the riddle below.

G. $\begin{array}{r} 32 \\ \times\ 48 \\ \hline \end{array}$
T. $\begin{array}{r} 67 \\ \times\ 14 \\ \hline \end{array}$
S. $\begin{array}{r} 53 \\ \times\ 27 \\ \hline \end{array}$
I. $\begin{array}{r} 96 \\ \times\ 52 \\ \hline \end{array}$
A. $\begin{array}{r} 83 \\ \times\ 33 \\ \hline \end{array}$
D. $\begin{array}{r} 49 \\ \times\ 72 \\ \hline \end{array}$

M. $\begin{array}{r} 39 \\ \times\ 28 \\ \hline \end{array}$
E. $\begin{array}{r} 56 \\ \times\ 15 \\ \hline \end{array}$
N. $\begin{array}{r} 83 \\ \times\ 24 \\ \hline \end{array}$
R. $\begin{array}{r} 75 \\ \times\ 46 \\ \hline \end{array}$
K. $\begin{array}{r} 96 \\ \times\ 51 \\ \hline \end{array}$
H. $\begin{array}{r} 84 \\ \times\ 62 \\ \hline \end{array}$

What horses like to stay up late?

$\overline{\hspace{1cm}}$ $\overline{\hspace{1cm}}$ $\overline{\hspace{1cm}}$ $\overline{\hspace{1cm}}$ $\overline{\hspace{1cm}}$ $\overline{\hspace{1cm}}$ $\overline{\hspace{1cm}}$ $\overline{\hspace{1cm}}$ $\overline{\hspace{1cm}}$ $\overline{\hspace{1cm}}$!

1,992   4,992   1,536   5,208   938   1,092   2,739   3,450   840   1,431

 Each of Farmer Gray's 24 horses eat 68 pounds of hay. How many pounds of hay do the horses eat altogether?

When a multiplication problem involves money, the product must have a dollar sign and a decimal point. The decimal point is placed between the ones digit and the tenths digit.

```
    6
    2
  $3.71
x     94
  14.84
+ 333.90
 $348.84
```

Remember to use a dollar sign and a decimal point.

Multiply. Then use the code to answer the riddle below.

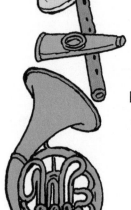

N. $1.94 x 23   **M.** $0.79 x 25   **I.** $2.06 x 64   **O.** $0.68 x 45

A. $3.68 x 32   **T.** $9.54 x 19   **F.** $0.88 x 72   **D.** $0.93 x 94

E. $8.15 x 67   **S.** $7.43 x 92   **R.** $0.87 x 75   **H.** $6.92 x 83

Where do musicians buy instruments?

___ ___ $117.76 $181.26 $181.26 $574.36 $546.05

___ $63.36 $131.84 $63.36 $546.05 $117.76 $44.62 $87.42

___ $87.42 $131.84 $19.75 $546.05 $683.56 $181.26 $30.60 $65.25 $546.05 !

Scholastic

To divide with zeros, follow these samples.

$$\begin{array}{r} 80 \\ 8\overline{)640} \end{array}$$
$64 \div 8 = 8$
$0 \div 8 = 0$
Add a zero to make 80.

$$\begin{array}{r} 800 \\ 8\overline{)6400} \end{array}$$
$64 \div 8 = 8$
$0 \div 8 = 0$
$0 \div 8 = 0$
Add 2 zeros to make 800.

Divide.

A. $6\overline{)420}$ $9\overline{)8100}$ $6\overline{)540}$ $5\overline{)4500}$ $3\overline{)2400}$

B. $3\overline{)1800}$ $4\overline{)320}$ $8\overline{)7200}$ $7\overline{)560}$ $5\overline{)400}$

C. $3\overline{)150}$ $4\overline{)360}$ $6\overline{)4800}$ $6\overline{)360}$ $8\overline{)640}$

Scholastic

A fraction consists of two parts.

 $\dfrac{3}{4}$ The **numerator** tells how many parts are being identified.
The **denominator** tells the total number of equal parts in the whole.

A.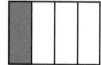

_____   _____   _____   _____   _____

B.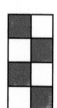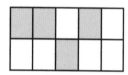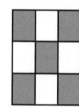

_____   _____   _____   _____   _____

C.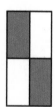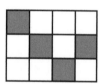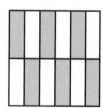

_____   _____   _____   _____   _____

Scholastic

Find the missing term to make each pair of fractions equivalent.

Example: $\dfrac{2}{4} = \dfrac{8}{16}$

1. $\dfrac{3}{4} = \dfrac{15}{}$ **2.** $\dfrac{4}{6} = \dfrac{12}{}$ **3.** $\dfrac{5}{8} = \dfrac{}{32}$ **4.** $\dfrac{4}{9} = \dfrac{16}{}$

5. $\dfrac{3}{5} = \dfrac{}{25}$ **6.** $\dfrac{3}{11} = \dfrac{9}{}$ **7.** $\dfrac{8}{9} = \dfrac{}{27}$ **8.** $\dfrac{3}{7} = \dfrac{}{21}$

9. $\dfrac{4}{5} = \dfrac{16}{}$ **10.** $\dfrac{2}{3} = \dfrac{}{9}$ **11.** $\dfrac{7}{10} = \dfrac{14}{}$ **12.** $\dfrac{5}{6} = \dfrac{}{36}$

Find the missing terms in each row of fractions.

13. $\dfrac{1}{3} = \dfrac{}{6} = \dfrac{}{9} = \dfrac{}{12} = \dfrac{}{15}$

14. $\dfrac{3}{4} = \dfrac{}{8} = \dfrac{}{12} = \dfrac{12}{} = \dfrac{15}{}$

15. $\dfrac{2}{3} = \dfrac{}{6} = \dfrac{6}{} = \dfrac{}{12} = \dfrac{10}{}$

16. $\dfrac{4}{5} = \dfrac{8}{} = \dfrac{}{15} = \dfrac{}{20} = \dfrac{20}{}$

Scholastic

Solve each of the problems below. Fill in the cross-number puzzle with the answers you've written on the lines next to the questions (2 D = 2 Down; 3 A = 3 Across). Look at the numbers you've written in the shaded boxes. Each number shows where the letter in that box should go in the code boxes at the bottom to answer the riddle.

Whose head is always in the stars?

1. The Ringling Bros. and Barnum & Bailey circus can boast of having two of the largest circus audiences ever. An audience of 52,385 attended the circus at the Superdome in New Orleans, Louisiana, and a tent audience of 16,702 was recorded in Concordia, Kansas.

• How much larger was the audience at the Superdome that the one in the tent?   _____ = 2 D

• What's the combined total audience that saw the circus at the Superdome and in a tent?   _____ = 4 D

2. An estimated 48,000 people took part in a Chicken Dance in Cincinnati, Ohio.

• How many more people attended the circus at the Superdome (see problem 1) than the Chicken Dance in Cincinnati?   _____ = 3 A

• By how much did the participants at the Chicken Dance outnumber those that were in a tent audience in Kansas?   _____ = 2 A

3. The Coliseum in Rome, Italy, was completed in A.D. 80 and could hold 87,000 spectators.

• How many more people could have attended an event at the Coliseum than the circus at the Superdome (see problem 1)?   _____ = 1 A

• In order to have the same number of spectators as the Coliseum, how many more Chicken Dance participants would be needed (see problem 2)?   _____ = 5 A

4. The Warwick Farm Racecourse in Australia had a record attendance at an Australia Day Bar-B-Que of 44,158 people.

• If all of these people wanted to be part of the tent audience in Concordia (see problem 1), how many people would not be able to get in for the first performance?   _____ = 6 A

• How many more Bar-B-Que participants would be needed in order to match the number of participants in the Chicken Dance (see problem 2)?   _____ = 1 D

AN [_][_][_][_][_][_][_][_][_][_] 'S
  1 2 3 4 5 6 7 8 9 0

Scholastic

Answer Key

READING/LANGUAGE ARTS

The Alphabet in Cursive

Pages 14–45

Review tracing, copying, and cursive writing on each page.

Pages 46–47

1. H   2. A   3. D   4. H   5. B

Spelling

Page 49

1. bib; tot   2. solos; did   3. pup; Hannah
4. noon; dad   5. gag; Bob   6. pop; Madam
7. toot; Otto   8. race car; Ava   9. kayak; refer
10. eve; Anna   11. mum; Mom   12. dud; Nan

Page 50

A. short a: dragon, dance, handle
ai: plains, raise, wait
a_e: brave, mistake, became
ay: today, maybe, holiday
B. mistake, raise, holiday, became

Page 51

A. holiday, wait, brave, dragon, dance, maybe
B. 1. mistake   2. raise   3.dance   4. became
5. today   6. plains   7. handle   FIREBALL
C. costume, parade, balloons

Page 52

A. short e: member, next, check, enter
ea: scream, reason, reach, team
ee: cheek, freeze, asleep, between
B. scream, cheek, freeze, check

Page 53

A. 1. enter   2. scream   3. freeze   4. team
5. member   6. asleep
B. Across: scream, member, cheek
Backward: check, team, asleep
Down: between, reach, enter
Diagonally: next, reason, freeze
C. 7. big ball; soccer   8. chess; tennis
9. ball; basketball

Page 54

A. short i: winter, middle, kitchen, children
i_e: surprise, polite, while, strike
gh: bright, frighten, tight, slight
B. surprise, polite, while, strike

Page 55

A. 1. polite   2. strike   3. surprise   4. kitchen
5. children   6. winter
B. 7. middle   8. bright   9. slight   10. surprise
11. tight   12. while   13. kitchen   14. strike
15. polite   C. 16. igloo   17. sleigh   18. icicle

Page 56

A. short o: rocket, monster, holler, bottle
o_e: alone, globe, whole, suppose
ow: pillow, below, window
short o and ow: follow
B. pillow, follow, holler, bottle

Page 57

A. pillow, rocket, holler, window, whole, bottle, suppose
B. 1. globe   2. below   3. whole   4. holler
5. pillow   6. bottle   7. suppose   8. follow
9. rocket   10. window   11. alone   12. monster
C. 1. blanket   2. feather   3. trouble

Page 58

A. short u: until, number, sudden
long u: super, ruler, duty
oo: loose, shampoo, caboose
ou: coupon, group, soup
B. coupon, ruler, shampoo, soup, caboose, number, group, duty

Page 59

A. 1. coupon   2. ruler   3. group   4. loose
5. shampoo   6. until   CEREAL
B. 7. caboose, number   8. coupon, loose
9. super, soup   10. sudden, duty   11. group, until;   C. supermarket, groceries, shopping

Page 60

A. au: because, pause, sauce, author
aw: hawk, awful, dawn, crawl
augh: daughter, naughty, caught, taught
B. Review student's choices.

Page 61

A. author, because, caught, dawn, pause, hawk, taught;   B. 1. caught   2. crawl
3. naughty   4. daughter   5. taught   6. sauce
7. awful;   C. Review that directions have been followed.

Page 62

geraff, larg, jentle, fense, senter, danjer, gienf, stranje
A. c as /s/: office, excite, fence, center, since, price; g as /j/: giant, giraffe, strange, gentle, danger, large;   B. giant, strange, gentle, large

Page 63

A. giraffe, large, gentle, fence, center, danger, giant, strange;   B. 1. large   2. office   3. gentle
4. strange   5. danger   6. excite   7. since
8. price; GIGANTIC;   C. monkey, antelope, elephant

Page 64

A. -er: swimmer, safer, freezer
-est: wisest, biggest, whitest
-ed: hoped, clapped, stopped
-ing: shopping, getting, coming
B. wisest, hoped, safer, freezer, whitest

Page 65

A. 1. biggest; double the final consonant
2. hoped; drop the silent e
3. coming; drop the silent e
4. getting; double the final consonant
5. whitest; drop the silent e
6. wisest; drop the silent e
B. 1. coming   2. shopping   3. clapped
4. stopped   5. swimmer   6. freezer   7. hoped
8. safer; COLD MEDAL
C. medal, compete, champion

Page 66

A. Review ideas;   B. Review choices.

Page 67

A. 1. these   2. done   3. favorite   4. friend
5. before   6. always   7. their   8. people
9. thought   10–12. does, done, been
13. always   14. their   15. favorite   16. other
17. people   18. friend;   C. 19. animal; mammal
20. kind; breed   21. dogs; canines

Page 68

A. our: court, pour, fourth, course
ear: search, pearl, Earth, early
ur: purse, turtle, burn, hurry
B. search, pour, burn, hurry, purse, court, course

Page 69

A. 1. search   2. pour   3. turtle   4. early
5. Earth   6. pearl   7. purse   8. course
B. 9. court   10. course   11. turtle   12. purse
13. pearl   14. hurry   15. fourth   16. burn
7. early;   C. 18. octopus   19. seashell   20. oyster

Page 70

A. air: fair, stairs, repair, chair
are: rare, share, scare, careful
ear: pear, tear, bear, wear
B. Review that directions have been followed.

Page 71

A. rare, pear, fair, bear, careful, chair, tear
B. 1. careful   2. repair   3. fair   4. pear
5A. stairs   5D. share   6. scare   7. chair
8. wear   9. bear   10. rare;   C. 1. o-range
2. pine-ap-ple   3. wa-ter-me-lon

Pages 73–76

1. B   2. G   3. C   4. D   5. J   6. C   7. C   8. G
9. A   10. D   11. J   12. D

Reading Skills & Reading Comprehension

Page 79
1. Alexander Graham Bell 2. teacher of the deaf
3. "Mr. Watson, come here! I want to see you!"
4. his assistant 5. Bell demonstrated his invention to many people.

Page 80
Main idea: galaxy; 1. stars 2. outer 3. spiral
4. white 5. sun 6. billions

Page 81
1. circle: wow, dad, mom, noon, deed
X: funny, tall 2. screech, pow, slurp, boom, click, sizzle, crunch 3. knot/not, break/brake, flu/flew, sore/soar, right/write, rode/road
4. pear, shoe, soccer, like, hen, neither

Page 82
7, 4, 8, 1, 5, 3, 6, 2

Page 83
4, 6, 1, 3, 5, 2

Page 84
1. Potato chips were invented by accident.
2. George Crum was a chef in Saratoga Springs.
3. The complaining diner actually caused something good to happen.
4. Mr. Crum was angry when the diner sent his potatoes back, but he was probably glad later on because his chips became famous.
5. Saratoga Chips were named after the town where they were invented.
6. The reason we have potato chips today is because of what happened at Moon's Lake House in 1853.

Page 85
1. deserves 2. sign 3. dirty 4. all together
5. change 6. burned 7. color 8. hide

Page 86
1. enough 2. save 3. gleaming 4. think about
5. send 6. top 7. injured 8. blow up

Page 87
1. on a roller coaster 2. in a candy store
3. in a movie theater 4. in an airplane
5. at the veterinarian's office

Page 88
1. eyedrops, aspirin, bandages, cough syrup
2. quilts, blankets, pillowcases, sheets
3. teaspoons, forks, serving spoons, knives
4. cake mix, crackers, cereal, canned soup
5. motor oil, car wax, fishing tackle, toolbox
6. encyclopedias, dictionary, atlas, novels

Page 89
1. views 2. views 3. news 4. views 5. news
6. news 7. views 8. news 9. views

Page 90
1. O, F 2. O, F 3. O, F 4. F, O 5. O, O, F, F, F

Page 91

B. 1. hockey 2. football 3. soccer 4. tennis
5. baseball 6. golf 7. basketball

Page 93
2. dwarf lantern shark 3. great white shark
4. mako shark 5. all 6. all
7. goblin shark 8. hammerhead shark
9. all 10. cookie cutter shark 11. sawshark
12. tiger shark

Page 95
1. B 2. E, D, A 3. G 4. F 5. C, F

Page 96
Shaky line: 1, 3, 4, 6, 8, 9

Page 97
1. a 2. boats 3. if they need to go far away and they want to get there quickly 4. to faraway lands 5. you can see the earth from way up high 6. car, van, bus, submarine, boat

Page 99
1. D 2. H 3. Neil Armstrong, Buzz Aldrin
4. B 5. Review summary.

Page 101
1. A 2. J 3. B 4. H 5. used a different voice, put on funny noses or hats 6. Review opinion.

Page 103
1. sea turtle, tortoise 2. B 3. J
4. leatherback; weighs 1000 pounds 5. A

Pages 104–107
1. A 2. G 3. C 4. A 5. G 6. C
7. A 8. G 9. A 10. C 11. J 12. B

Vocabulary

Page 109
1. wallet; clothes 2. comma; parts of speech
3. earthquake; weather conditions
4. square; solid geometric shapes
5. Pacific; continents
6. banana; round fruits 7. daffodil; trees
8. swimming; sports with balls 9. open; computer keys 10. palm; parts of the eye

Page 110
1. pop 2. phon 3. pos 4. port 5. photo
6–10. Review definitions.

Page 111

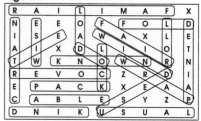

1. unusual 2. unfamiliar 3. untie 4. unlock
5. unfold 6. unwise 7. unpack 8. unfair

Page 112
Review definitions and refer to dictionary while focusing on the following prefixes and root words: 1. away from; to carry
2. forward; to put 3. before; to say
4. into; to put 5. before; to come
6. against; to say 7. around; to come
8. into; to carry

Page 113
Review definitions and refer to dictionary while focusing on the following prefixes and root words: 1. away from; to break 2. across; to put 3. between; to throw 4. up; to go
5. from; to put 6. forward; to go 7. through; to put 8. forward; to push

Page 114
Review definitions and refer to dictionary while focusing on the following suffixes and root words: 1. life; result of 2. to do; a state of 3. believe; ability 4. to do; a state of; a person 5. empty; a state of 6. true; a state of
7. year; result of 8. short; a state of

Page 115
A. 1. hive, dive, five 2. head, bed, sled
3. cove, drove, rove 4. bleed, feed, weed
5. find, hind, mind B.1. b 2. a

Page 116
1. a, b 2. b, a 3. b, a 4. a, b 5. a, b 6. b, a

Page 117
1. board, bored 2. bear, bare 3. chili, chilly
4. raze, raise 5. guessed, guest 6. patience, patients 7. I'll meet you at eight in the morning. 8. Would you be a dear and fix me some tea and a bowl of cereal? 9. My aunt and uncle lived overseas for two years in Madrid, the capital city of Spain. 10. Alex was sick with the flu for four days and missed a whole week of school. 11. I want to buy a new pair of shoes, but I do not have a cent left. 12. We'd better put away the pie before Harry eats it all.

Page 118
A. some/sum, way/weigh, flower/flour, close/clothes, hear/here, wood/would
B. flower, flour, close, clothes

Scholastic

Page 119
A. 1. weigh 2. sum 3. flour 4. clothes
5. hear 6. close; B. 7. sum 8. wood, weigh
9. flower, here 10. close, flour 11. Would
12. way, here 13. some, clothes;
C. 1. cookies 2. sprinkles 3. sugar

Page 120
1. bark 2. leaf 3. stem 4. root 5. trunk
6. trunk, j 7. bark, b 8. root, g 9. stem, e
9. leaf, d

Page 121
1. absent; absent 2. cheap; expensive
3. arrive; depart 4. trust; trust 5. freeze;
melt 6. reduce; reduce 7. public; private
8. seldom; often 9. group; individual
10. sharp; sharp

Page 122
1A. tasteless 1D. timid 2. safe 3. stingy
4. calm 5. few 6. rude 7. unknown 8. silly
9. unclear 10. tiny 11. careless

Page 123
1. young; full-grown 2. powerful; needed
3. smart; thin 4. thin; overweight 5. full-
grown; pleasant 6. empty; enormous
7. pleasant; bold 8. needed; crowded
9. crowded; empty 10. bold; smart
11. overweight; powerful 12. enormous; young

Page 124
1. kn; on a door 2. wr; in a toolbox
3. c; in an orchestra 4. ph; in an album
5. sch; in a classroom 6. gn; at a zoo
7. wr; at a birdfeeder 8. gn; in a fairy tale
9. kn; in your body 10. kn; on a shelf
11. gh; in a scary movie 12. x; in a marching band;
EXTRA: L

Page 125
schoolhouse, schoolwork, schoolroom,
backside, background, fallout, doorstep,
sidestep, underside, underwater, underground,
fireside, firehouse, fireproof, waterfall,
waterproof, footstep, footprint, footwork,
storeroom, townhouse, downfall, downtown,
downtime, workout, outback, outhouse,
breakdown, breakout, groundwater, printout,
meantime; B. 1. printout 2. background
3. waterproof 4. townhouse 5. footwork

Page 126
A. 1 spring + time 2. some + one
3. birth + day 4. after + noon 5. out + doors
6. every + thing 7. home + work
8. skate + board 9. note + book
10. break + fast 11. blue + bird 12. up + stairs
B. afternoon, outdoors, everything, upstairs

Page 127
A. springtime, outdoors, homework, upstairs,
notebook, bluebird, skateboard
B. homework, skateboard, upstairs, notebook,
bluebird, breakfast, someone, everything,
birthday, afternoon, springtime, outdoors
C. grasshopper, ladybug, butterfly

Page 128
1. edition 2. thorough 3. umpire 4. costume
5. quiet 6. biography 7. commend 8. finely
9. than 10. area

Page 129
1. accept 2. dessert 3. angles 4. finale
5. breath 6. loose 7. calendar 8. pasture
9. comma 10. picture

Page 130
1. German 2. African 3. Dutch 4. Dutch
5. Turkish 6. Italian 7. Russian 8. Spanish
9. French 10. Yiddish 11. French 12. Japanese

Page 131
States, National Symbols, Inventors,
Landforms, Leaders, Nations, Explorers, Map,
Government, Mountain Ranges, Cities, Oceans

Page 132

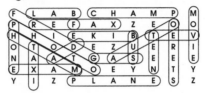

Page 133
1. brain 2A. lungs 2D. liver 3. stomach
4. esophagus 5. intestines 6. heart 7. trachea

Page 134
1. musician 2. melody 3. composer 4. opera
5. orchestra 6. woodwind 7. conductor
8. rhythm; SYMPHONY

Page 135
1. inventor 2. century 3. continent
4. communication 5. south 6. state
7. nation 8. consumer 9. demand 10. elect
11. resolution 12. immigrant EXTRA: 5

Page 136
1. mechanic is to cars 2. kilogram is to scale
3. patient is to physician 4. lost is to found
5. gasoline is to gas 6. borough is to burrow
7. gram is to g 8. koala is to eucalyptus leaves
9. hire is to fire 10. spaghetti is to Italian

Pages 143–144
1. D 2. H 3. A 4. B 5. G 6. D

Grammar/Writing

Page 146
1. S 2. F 3. S 4. S 5. F 6. S 7. S 8. F 9. F
10. F 11. S 12. S

Page 147
A. 1. Q 2. S 3. S 4. Q 5. Q 6. F 7. S 8. Q
B. 1. How did the ant carry the crumb?
2. She carried it herself.

Page 148
A. 1. E 2. C 3. C 4. E 5. E 6. C 7. E 8. C
B. Review that your child composes sentences
that are the following: 1. exclamation
2. command 3. exclamation 4. exclamation
5. command 6. command 7. command

Page 149
A. 1. class, took 2. paintings, hung
3. Maria, saw 4. children, looked
5. Paul, pointed 6. friend, liked
7. everyone, laughed 8. people, visited
9. bus, took B. Review sentences.

Page 150
A. 1. Mike and Jody; CS 2. call and email; CP
3. jogs and swims; CP 4. Phil and Jan; CS
5. Juan and Yoshi; CS 6. speak and read; CP
7. Lori, Sam, and Beth; CS 8. practiced and
presented; CP 9. clapped and smiled; CP
10. The parents and the principal; CS
B. 1. barked and jumped 2. My dad and sister

Page 151
A. 1. S 2. S 3. P 4. S 5. P; B. 1. baby; sisters
2. nightgown; pockets 3. hand; fingers
4. baby; parents 5. family; girls
C. fences, train, gates, cow

Page 152
A. 1. doctor, Pat 2. park, Atlanta 3. football,
Tangram; B. Review that directions have been
followed.

Page 153
A. 1. Anna's; S 2. birds'; P 3. Brad's; S
4. butterfly's; S 5. turtle's; S 6. chipmunks'; P
7. animals'; P B. 1. Carol's 2. Jim's 3. sister's
4. brother's 5. dad's 6. sneaker's 7. dog's

Page 154
A. 1. He; S 2. I; S 3. They; P 4. We; P 5. It; S
B. 1. It; story; singular 2. she; author; singular
3. We; My friends and I; plural 4. They; Two
boys; P C. 1. it 2. it 3. they 4. she

Page 155
A. 1. us 2. it 3. him 4. you 5. me 6. her
7. them B. 1. them 2. her 3. it 4. him
5. us; C. Review sentences for a subject
pronoun and a predicate pronoun.

Page 156
A. 2. you; your 3. he; his 4. she; her
5. it; its 6. we; our 7. they; their
B. 1. their 2. her 3. his 4. his 5. my 6. your
7. its 8. our

Page 157
A. 1. cheered 2. added 3. give 4. serves
5. emptied; B. 1. paraded 2. whispered
3. gobbled 4. skipped 5. bounced;
C. 1. laughed 2. sighed 3. whispered

Page 158
A. 1. fills 2. watches 3. takes 4. leave 5. go
B. 1. looked 2. stared 3. walked 4. helped
C. Review sentences.

Page 159
A. 1. was 2. is 3. are 4. am 5. were
B. 1. past 2. present 3. present 4. past
5. present; C. 1. am 2. are 3. is

Scholastic

Page 160
A. 1. had; built   2. has; painted   3. is; building
4. will; fly   5. will; bring   6. am; buying
B. 1. is   2. had   3. going   4. using   5. will
6. have; C. Review sentences.

Page 161
A. 1. told   2. was   3. came   4. saw   5. knew
6. fell   7. lit   8. threw; B. 1. knew   2. saw
3. threw   4. fell; C. Review that sentences
include "knew" and "told".

Page 162
1. sparkling   2. clear   3. large   4. busy   5. fresh
B. Review sentences for adjectives.

Page 163
a. 1. the, the   2. an   3. a, a, a   4. an   5. the,
the, the   6. the, a   7. the, an, the   8. an, the
B. 1. a   2. the   3. the   4. an   5. an   6. the
7. a   8. a

Page 164
A. 1. where is   2. would not   3. you will
4. have not   5. we have   6. she is
7. they will   8. should not   9. that is
10. you have   11. does not   12. are not
B. you'll, we've, they'll, you've

Page 165
A. 1. wouldn't   2. she's   3. doesn't   4. they'll
5. you've   6. haven't

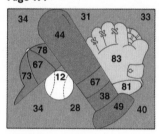

C. Review definitions.

Page 166
A. 1. it's   2. we're   3. they've   4. I'm   5. she'll
6. they're; B. 1. I've; I have   2. What's; what is
3. it's; it is   4. they're; they are   5. I'm; I am
C. 1. he'll   2. they're   3. who's   4. I'm   5. we'll
6. there's

Page 167
A. 1. "I have a strange case,"   2. "What's
strange about it?"   3. "Seventeen years ago
Mr. Hunt found an elephant,"   4. "Where did
he find it?"   5. " The elephant just appeared
in the window,"   6. "He must have fainted!"
7. "No, Mr. Hunt bought him,"
B. 1. Huntsville, Alabama   2. 12 Oak Street,
Huntsville, Alabama   3. January 8, 2001
4. January 22, 2001   5. 75 Peachtree Lane,
Farley, Alabama   6. Redstone Park, Alabama
7. September 29, 2000   8. 47 Draper Road,
Newportville, Pennsylvania

Page 168
Sentences may vary. 1. The melting snow cone
sat in the bright sun.   2. Many excited
children ran toward the crashing ocean waves
3. My new friends built a large sandcastle   4.
My younger brother grabbed his favorite
beach toys.   5. Our playful dog tried to catch
flying beach balls.

Page 169
2. I like salt and ketchup on my French fries.
3. My mom makes great pork chops and
applesauce.   4. My dad eats two huge
helpings of meat loaf and potatoes!
5. My brother helps set the table and clean
the dishes.   6. We have cookies and ice cream
for dessert.

Page 170
Review that sentences correspond with
questions.

Page 171
Review that topic sentences correspond with
following sentences.

Page 172
1. My favorite kind of dog is a boxer.
2. Not much is known about the history
of Chinese flags.
3. Hurricanes have strong, powerful winds.

Page 173
Review paragraphs for 3 supporting sentences.

Page 174
Review that paragraphs include a clear
beginning, middle, and ending.

Page 175
Review closing sentences.

Page 176
Review plan and paragraph.

Page 177
Review plan and persuasive paragraph.

Page 178
Review plan and expository paragraph.

Page 179
Review letter for necessary parts.

Pages 180–183
1. D   2. J   3. A   4. D   5. H   6. D   7. B   8. F
9. B   10. C   11. F   12. B

Addition & Subtraction
Page 185
2. 18, 16, 14   3. 18, 15, 17   4. 8, 18, 15
5. 18, 9,15   6. 12, 9, 18   7. 16, 11, 17   8. 13, 11,
18   9. 14, 18, 16   10. 4, 9, 2; BONUS 13 ships

Page 186
1. 14, 8, 2, 5, 1; 2. 2, 7, 11; 3. 4, 2, 5, 1,1 7
4. 14, 2, 10, 11, 4
Spade, axe, radio, saber; cross out *radio*

Page 187
1. 7, a   2. 14, g   3. 9, c   4. 18, b   5. 11, e   6. 13, f
7. 5, d   8. 17, j   9. 10, i   10. 6, k   11. 12, h
12. 8, l   13. 15, m

Page 188
1. 75, 23, 98, 86, 47, 34, 75, 99
2. 86, 98, 33, 78, 64, 87, 32, 47, 78, 99
3. 64, 47, 51, 98, 86, 32, 21   4. 51, 98, 64, 64
AMERICAN REVOLUTION LIBERTY BELL

Page 189
1. 52, 53, 82, 61, 96, 52, 82; LINCOLN
2. 37, 83, 42, 42, 83, 78, 64, 96, 82; JEFFERSON
3. 98, 72, 64, 65, 53, 82, 45, 47, 96, 82;
WASHINGTON

Page 190
1. 45, 28, 19, 74, 65; 2. 53, 79, 37, 38, 66

Page 191

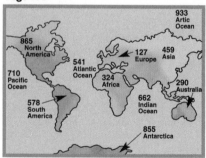

Pattern: 38, 40, 44, 48, 50

Page 192
1. 2, 9 ,5   2. 1, 5, 9   3. 1, 3, 6   4. 1, 3, 6
5. 5, 2, 7   6. 1, 6, 8   7. 0, 2, 4   8. 4, 2, 2
9. 4, 2, 5   10. 5, 4, 7   11. 5, 3, 3   12. 7, 3, 4
13. 0, 5, 3   14. 1, 3, 8   15. 4, 3, 7   16. 4, 2, 4
EXTRA: Joe had $5.40 and Ellie had $4.35

Page 193
1. 574, 534, 558; 2. 346, 506, 763; 3. 852, 523,
945; 4. 952, 524, 965; 5. 897, 563, 723; "T"
6. 726, 622, 923; 7. 327, 288, 525; 8. 628, 824,
421; 9. 826, 842, 428; 10. 724, 725, 527; "B"

Page 194
1. d   2. b   3. i   4. f   5. g   6. e   7. a   8. h   9. c

Page 195
A. 496 – 188 = 308   B. 956 – 668 = 288
C. 547 + 239 = 786   D. 379 + 345 = 724
E. 723 – 162 = 561   F. 422 – 215 = 207
G. 957 – 688 = 269   H. 884 + 834 = 1718
I. 956 – 578 = 378; EXTRA: Orange: 956, 957;
Purple: 162, 188

Page 196

EXTRA: 2,846

Scholastic

Page 197

1. 5,063   2. 3,721   3. 3,827   4. 8,749
5. 8,789   6. 2,429   7. 3,012   8. 5,642
9. 2,351   10. 2,429   11. 5,234   12. 5,063
13. 8,789   14. 5,642   15. 5,063   16. 6,348
17. 4,907   18. 7,483   19. 8,749
ALPS, ROCKY, OZARK, ANDES

Page 198

1. d   2. a   3. f   4. b   5. g   6. c   7. e

Page 199

1. c   2. d   3. a   4. e   5. f   6. b

Page 200

1. 5,160   2. 5,737   3. 1,851   4. 3,685
5. 6,588   6. 8,557   7. 6,620   8. 7,062
9. 7,371   10. 2,887   11. 5,763   12. 6,231
MATH IS AWESOME!

Page 201

1. 15   2. 19   3. 14   4. 18   5. 17
6. 27   7. 40   8. 26   9. 38   10. 47
11. 68   12. 83
Review strategy for making easy numbers.

Page 202

1. 22   2. 27   3. 43   4. 45   5. 80
6. 97   7. 62   8. 114   9. 140   10. 190
11. 60   12. 93   13. 140   14. 362   15. 442
Review strategy for solving Problem 12.

Pages 203–205

1. B   2. J   3. B   4. H   5. B   6. H
7. B   8. J   9. B   10. H   11. A   12. G

Multiplication & Division

Page 207

A. 4, 9, 12; B. 12, 18, 21; C. 14, 18, 10;
D. 2, 24, 10, 0, 6, 14; E. 8, 9, 3, 12, 0, 3

Page 208

1. 12   2. 4   3. 8   4. 32   5. 28   6. 30
7. 15   8. 5   9. 16   10. 25   11. 0   12. 10
13. 20   14. 45   15. 36   16. 24   17. 35   18. 40
19. SIRIUS AND CANOPUS

Page 209

x4: 32, 20, 12, 28, 16, 24, 36
x2: 12, 8, 6, 10, 14, 4, 18, 16
x3: 27, 6, 12, 15, 9, 21, 18, 24
x5: 15, 45, 25, 35, 10, 20, 30, 40
EXTRA: 36 miles

Page 210

1. sixteen   2A. thirty-six   2D. thirty-two
3. forty-eight   4. twenty   5. eight
6. twenty-four   7. twelve   8. twenty-eight
9. forty   10. four   11. zero   12. forty-four
EXTRA: 44 buttons

Page 211

A. 10   B. 1   C. 7   D. 50   E. 12   F. 30   G. 11
H. 15   I. 40   J. 9   K. 5   L. 5   M. 35   N. 60
O. 4; EXTRA: 60 nuts

Page 212

Page 213

40, 72, 18, 24, 36, 48, 8, 81, 32, 56, 54, 64, 27,
16, 0, 45; EXTRA: 16 cubs

Page 214

A. 54, 72, 40, 48, 24   B. 27, 81, 56, 18, 32
C. 72, 0, 16, 64, 54   D. 36, 63, 9, 32, 0
E. 27, 40, 63, 8, 45; EXTRA: Circle: 24 in
Row A, 18 in Row B, 16 in Row C, 9 in Row D,
8 in Row E

Page 215

1. forty-five   2. twenty-seven   3. fifty-four
4. zero   5. nine   6. seventy-two   7. one
hundred eight   8. sixty-three   9. thirty-six
10. ninety   11. eighty-one   12. eighteen
13. ninety-nine; EXTRA:108 pieces

Page 216

255, 48, 368, 126, 28, 48, 219, 166, 88, 244,
102, 126; EXTRA: 96 laps

Page 217

A. 144, 125, 441; B. 664, 432, 116, 282, 385;
C. 310, 192, 290, 147, 384

Page 218

N. 204   C. 51   A. 184   H. 310   I. 318   B. 504
S. 112   K. 96   R. 108   B. 117
IN BRANCH BANKS

Page 219

A. 628, 690   B. 1296, 2084
C. 1208, 2106   D. 2169, 1842, 482, 2439
E. 336, 248, 909, 2480

Page 220

A. 2,835   B. 1,824   C. 3,375   D. 5,348
E. 1,752   F. 2,904   G. 1,564   H. 3,192
I. 3,232   J. 2,430

Page 221

A. 3 x 78 = 234   B. 8 x 2 = 16
C. 48 x 6 = 288   D. 3 x 265 = 795
E. 3 x 24 = 72   F. 4 x 5 = 20

Page 222

1. f   2. a   3. k   4. h   5. e   6. b
7. j   8. c   9. i   10. g   11. l   12. d

Page 223

10 ÷ 5 = 2; 10 ÷ 2 = 5

Page 224

A. 4   B. 2   C. 4   D. 5   E. 6   F. 3   G. 8   H. 5

Page 225

A. 3, 3, 5   B. 4, 7, 4   C. 1, 6, 8   D. 6, 7   E. 2, 1
F. 5, 8   G. 18 ÷ 6 = 3

Page 226

A. 6, 8, 9, 1   B. 9, 5, 5, 7   C. 2, 4, 8, 9, 5
D. 3, 7, 2, 3, 6   E. 3 kites; EXTRA: 9 kites of
each color

Page 227

A. 4, 9, 1, 6   B. 5, 3, 8, 2   C. 8, 4, 5   D. 3, 1, 8, 9
E. 5, 2, 4, 2

Page 228

A. 6, 9, 6   B. 4, 9, 8   C. 2, 8, 4   D. 7, 10, 7
E. 8 students   F. 4 monkeys

Page 229

Circle: 1, 3, 5, 6, 7, 10, 11, 12, 14
2 miles each day

Page 230

Girl's path: 2, 9, 5, 3, 1, 4, 6, 7, 0
Boy's path: 5, 4, 7, 8, 2, 3, 9, 10, 6
EXTRA: 9 miles

Page 231

1R4   B. 6R2, 9R1, 7R5, 6R5
C. 7R2, 7R1, 7R1, 6R6
D. 5R1, 6R2, 3R1, 5R2
EXTRA: 6

Page 232

A. 8R1, 8R4, 6R1, 9R2   B. 7R1, 6R1, 5R3, 5R1
C. 4R1, 5R1, 8R2, 7R1   D. 3R2, 3R1, 9R2, 5R6
E. 4R1, 6R3, 2R4, 6R2
EXTRA: 7 apples

Page 233

A. 4 with 2 left over   B. 6   C. 7   D. 2
E. 2   F. 9

Page 234

A. 22, 24, 31, 13   B. 32, 21, 34, 10
C. 33, 23, 40, 11

Page 235

A.29, 17 ,12, 18   B. 16, 12, 37, 23
C. 13, 19, 13, 15
EXTRA: 29 marbles

Page 236

A. 63, 24, 36, 35   B. 9, 18, 48, 81
C. 32, 21, 16, 18   D. 64, 9, 30, 7   E. 160, 90, 300
F. 420, 300, 80; EXTRA: 128 people

Page 237

A. Ellen   B. 162   C. 20   D. 48   E. 9   F. $4.00

Page 238

1. 36   2. 155   3. 248   4. 86   5. 96   6. 54
7. 180   8. 104   9. 168   10. 216   11. 6   12. 7
13. 6   14. 8   15. 13   16. 12   17. 15   18. 12
19. 16   20. 12; Review explanation.

Pages 239–241

1. A   2. F   3. A   4. G   5. C   6. H
7. D   8. H   9. B   10. H   11. A   12. F

Scholastic

Fractions & Graphs

Page 243
1. 3/6 2. 2/4 3. 3/8 4. 2/3 5. 3/4 6. 4/5
7. 5/6 8. 5/8

Page 244
1. 1/4 2. 1/3 3. 1/4 4. 1/2 5. 1/2
6. 1/4 7. 1/3 8. 1/2 9. 1/3

Page 245
Review that directions have been followed.

Page 246
A. 2, 1/2 B. 3, 2/3 C. 5, 1/2 D. 5, 2/3
E. 4, 1/2 F. 2, 5/6 G. 3, 1/2 H. 3, 1/3
I. 7, 1/2 J. 2, 3/4 K. 5, 1/3 L. 4, 1/4

Page 247

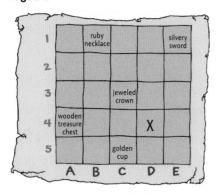

Page 248
1. Jan, Dec 2. 80° 3. Jun, Jul, Sep 4. yes, 10°
5. no 6. warmer 7. fall 8. May 9. 40°

Page 249
1. cheetah 2. black mamba snake 3. zebra
4. lion 5. 7 6. yes 7. speed 8. no

Page 250
1. 44, 8 2. 44, 36 3. 4, 36 4. 4, 8 5. 8, 12
6. 12, 16 7. 16, 20 8. 20, 24 9. 4, 36
10. 24, 20 11. 44, 36 12. 28, 24 13. 32, 20
14. 36, 16 15. 40, 12 16. 44, 8
CHALLENGE: a bee

Page 252
1. 4, 1 2. 9, 1 3. 9, 3 4. 2, 3 5. 8, 3 6. 8, 5
7. 8, 9 8. 6, 9 9. 6, 1 10. 7, 10 11. 6, 9
12. 4, 9 13. 4, 3; EXTRA: 4, 4, 10

Page 254
1. 77, 49 2. 70, 63 3. 63, 77 4. 49, 70
5. 35, 63 6. 42, 14 7. 14, 7 8. 21, 7 9. 21, 21
10. 28, 21 11. 28, 14 12. 21, 14 13. 14, 14
14. 14, 7; EXTRA: 35

Page 256
1. 11, 8 2. 10, 9 3. 2, 9 4. 1, 8 5. 6, 1 6. 9, 8
7. 8, 9 8. 6, 1 9. 3, 8 10. 4, 9 11. 6, 9
12. 5, 8 13. 6, 1 14. 7, 8 15. 6, 9; EXTRA: 12

Pages 258–260
1. B 2. H 3. C 4. F 5. B 6. J
7. D 8. A 9. H 10. D 11. H

Geometric Shapes, Time & Money

Page 262
1. 5 2. 13 3. 30 4. 12 5. 8 6. 17

Page 263
A. 1. F 2. G 3. B 4. A 5. J 6. I
7. E 8. H 9. G 10. G 11. C
B. 1. B 2. F 3. D 4. I 5. F 6. E
7. G 8. D 9. I 10. F 11. I
C. 1. C 2. C 3. C 4. G 5. G 6. C
7. F 8. I 9. B 10. C 11. F

Page 264
MEET YOU AT NOON

Page 265
1. 23, 7:23 2. 56, 10:56 3. 13, 5:13

Page 266
Review that directions have been followed.

Page 267
A. 0, 5, 10, 15, 20, 25, 30, 35, 40, 45, 50, 55
B. 2:25, 1:10, 3:35, 7:20, 8:55, 5:20

Page 268
1. 2:20 2. 5:50 3. 7:35 4. 1:25 5. 11:55
6. 12:50 7. 10:10 8. 4:05 9. 8:20 10. 4:10
11. 10:25

Page 269
1. one fifteen 2. seven forty-five
3. three o'clock 4. three thirty

Page 270
1. 5 pennies 2. 2 dimes 3. 1 quarter, 1 nickel
4. 3 dimes, 1 nickel 5. 1 quarter, 2 dimes
6. 1 quarter, 2 dimes, 1 nickel 7. 1 quarter,
1 dime, 1 nickel 8. 2 dimes, 1 nickel

Page 272
Review that directions have been followed.

Page 273
A variety of answers are possible. Review that directions have been followed

Page 274
1. b 2. c 3. a 4. 100 5. 20 6. 4
7. 50 8. 20 9. 100 10. 40

Page 275
1. $1.65 2. $5.36 3. $10.55 4. $6.25 5. $15.27

Pages 276–277
1. $4.25 2. $8.00 3. $6.25 4. $5.75
5. $3.50 6. $6.50 7. $6.50 8. $18.00
9. $4.00 10. Review strategy

Pages 278–280
1. C 2. G 3. C 4. H 5. A 6. G
7. D 8. G 9. C 10. H 11. C 12. G

GET READY FOR GRADE 4

Page 282
Nouns: moisture, council, boundary, downtown, mountain, allowance, oyster
Verbs: destroy, allow, avoid, employ, boiled, disappoint, found; Both: voyage

Page 283
1. found 2. mountain 3. oyster 4. avoid
5. allowance 6. employ 7. voyage 8. council
9. boiled 10. allow 11. moisture 12. boundary
13. disappoint 14. downtown 15. destroy

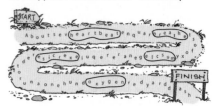

About seven quarts of oxygen are required to run a one hundred yard dash.

Page 284
atomic/freckle: attack, attic, clerk, cracker, frantic; handicap/picture: hawk, heroic, hockey, nickel, picnic; pink/trademark: plastic, rocket, shriek, stack, tractor

Page 285
A. 1. attack 2. hockey 3. hawk 4. attic
5. plastic 6. rocket 7. shriek 8. cracker, clerk
9. heroic, rocket 10. picnic, frantic
11. tractor, stack B. Olympic, competition, skiing, snowboarding, Athletes; skeleton

Page 286
Review definitions—refer to a dictionary.

Page 287
1. discontinued 2. disconnect 3. dishonest
4. disappear 5. discover 6. disagree,
disapprove 7. dislike 8. disobey

Page 288
1. eastward 2. heartily 3. resident
4. treacherous 5. American 6. government
7. zoology 8. necessity 9. noiseless
10. weaken 11. Washington

Page 289
1. conductor 2. professor 3. hairdresser
4. architect 5. custodian 6. paratrooper
7. astronaut 8. physician 9. geologist
10. cashier 11. archaeologist
12. astronomer

Page 290
A. 1. slurp 2. rumble 3. sizzle 4. crunched
5. thud 6. burp 7. crackled 8. clomped
9. screech 10. sputter B. Review sentences.

Page 291
1. shrimp 2. unfinished 3. half 4. bitter
5. serious 6. ugly 7. misunderstood 8. sorrow
9. whisper 10. minor 11. inside 12. original
13. estimate 14. random 15. awfully

Scholastic

Page 292
1. German 2. Hindi 3. Chinese 4. Dutch
5. French 6. Italian 7. Yiddish 8. Japanese
9. Spanish 10. Turkish 11. Yiddish 12. Spanish
13. Turkish 14. Italian 15. Spanish 16. French

Page 293
A. 1. before 2. then 3. when 4. after 5. soon
6. next 7. while 8. after 9. finally 10. now
B. 1. at last 2. after 3. then, first, next

Pages 294–295
Answers will vary. Sample main ideas: Letter one—Except for the bugs, Tyler and his new friends are having fun at camp.; Letter two—Tyler's mom is worried about his bug bites, and she wants him to start being nice to the other campers.; Letter three—Tyler is having a great time at camp, has some new friends, and is having fun playing tricks on other campers.; Letter four—Steven is sad he could not got to camp and remembers the fun he had at camp last year.

Page 297
1. hard worker, quick-acting, brave, fast-thinking 2. scared, alarmed, helpless
3. Review opinion. 4. B-good students, L-dependable, E-frightened, E-grateful, L-persistent, E-appreciative
5. Henry Heimlich 6. Mount Waialeale
7. just under 2" 8. Lindsay saved Erica's life by performing the Heimlich maneuver when Erica choked on her pen cap.

Page 299
1. B 2. H 3. Words that come from people's names 4. He loved to play cards and by making a sandwich he could eat without stopping his play. 5. Bloomers are pants that are worn under a dress. The word comes from the inventor's name, Amelia Bloomer.

Page 300
A 1. (of) mountains, rivers, and lakes
2. (on) the wall; (of) his room 3. (to) the scenes; (in) the pictures 4. (on) a camping trip
5. (in) a backpack and knapsack
6. (from) his father's mug 7. (in) the mountains; (for) hours 8. (at) the Lost Lake 9. (on) their journey 10. (at) a quiet place; (for) the night
11. (in) a tent 12. (from) the wind and rain
13. (to) his father 14. (on) their camping trip
B. Review sentences for prepositional phrases.

Page 301
Sentences may vary. 1. The Caspian Sea, covering an area about the same size as Montana, is the world's largest lake. 2. The Komodo dragon, growing to a length of 10 feet, is a member of the monitor family.
3. Our closest star, estimated to be more than 27,000,000° F, is the sun. 4. Ronald W. Reagan, a Hollywood actor for almost 30 years, was our nation's 40th president. 5. Georgia, harvesting over 2 billion pounds each year, is the state that grows the most peanuts. 6. Jackie Robinson, who played for the Brooklyn Dodgers, was the first African American to play in the major leagues.

Page 302
1. but 2. and 3. or 4. and 5. or 6. but
7. and 8. but 9. or 10. but 11. and 12. or
13. but 14. but

Page 303
Review that directions have been followed.

Page 304
1. 4,730 2. 2,405 3. 2,822 4. 7,920
5. 4,744 6. 6,132 7. 2,310 8. 6,845
9. 2,067 10. 9,128 11. 4,655 12. 3,173
13. 9,175 14. 4,236 15. 2,104 16. 5,870
17. 2,360 18. 4,578 19. 7,670 20. 1,857

Page 305
1. Z. 1,371; B. 632; R. 1,211; Q. 1,522; S. 1,201; X. 761
2. I. 9,107; C. 4,053; Y. 10,155; A. 14,024; Y. 9,122
3. L. 103,468; P. 76,076; E. 82,373; F. 92,228
4. D. 539,396; O. 651,951; R. 1,059,472
BIRDS OF PREY

Page 306
A. 560; 3000; 27,000; 440; 240; 12,000
B. 490; 36,000; 5,400; 42,000; 3,500; 360
C. 48,000; 480; 240; 4,500; 24,000; 400

Page 307
G. 1,536; T. 938; S. 1,431; I. 4,992; A. 2,739
D. 3,528; M. 1,092; E. 840; N. 1,992; R. 3,450
K. 4,896; H. 5,208; NIGHTMARES
EXTRA 1,632 pounds

Page 308
N. $44.62; M. $19.75; I. $131.84; O. $30.60
A. $117.76; T. $181.26; F. $63.36; D. $87.42
E. $546.05; S. $683.56; R. $65.25; H. $574.36
AT THE FIFE AND DIME STORE

Page 309
A. 70, 900, 90, 900, 800
B. 600, 80, 900, 80, 80
C. 50, 90, 800, 60, 80

Page 310
A. 1/4, 2/4, 1/2, 3/8, 1/3
B. 5/6, 4/8, 4/8, 4/10, 5/9
C. 1/5, 2/4, 2/6, 4/12, 6/12

Page 311
1. 20 2. 18 3. 20 4. 36 5. 15 6. 33 7. 24
8. 9 9. 20 10. 6 11. 20 12. 30 13. 2, 3, 4, 5;
14. 6, 9, 16, 20; 15. 4, 9, 8, 15; 16. 10, 12, 16, 25

Page 312
1A. 34,615 1D. 3,842 2A. 31,298 2D. 35,683
3. 4,385 4. 69,087 5. 39,000 6. 27,456
AN ASTRONOMER'S

Scholastic

Success with Reading & Math!

SCHOLASTIC

You're a Scholastic Superstar!

Grade 3 Jumbo Workbook

Scholastic

has completed the

_____

Presented on

_____

Congratulations!

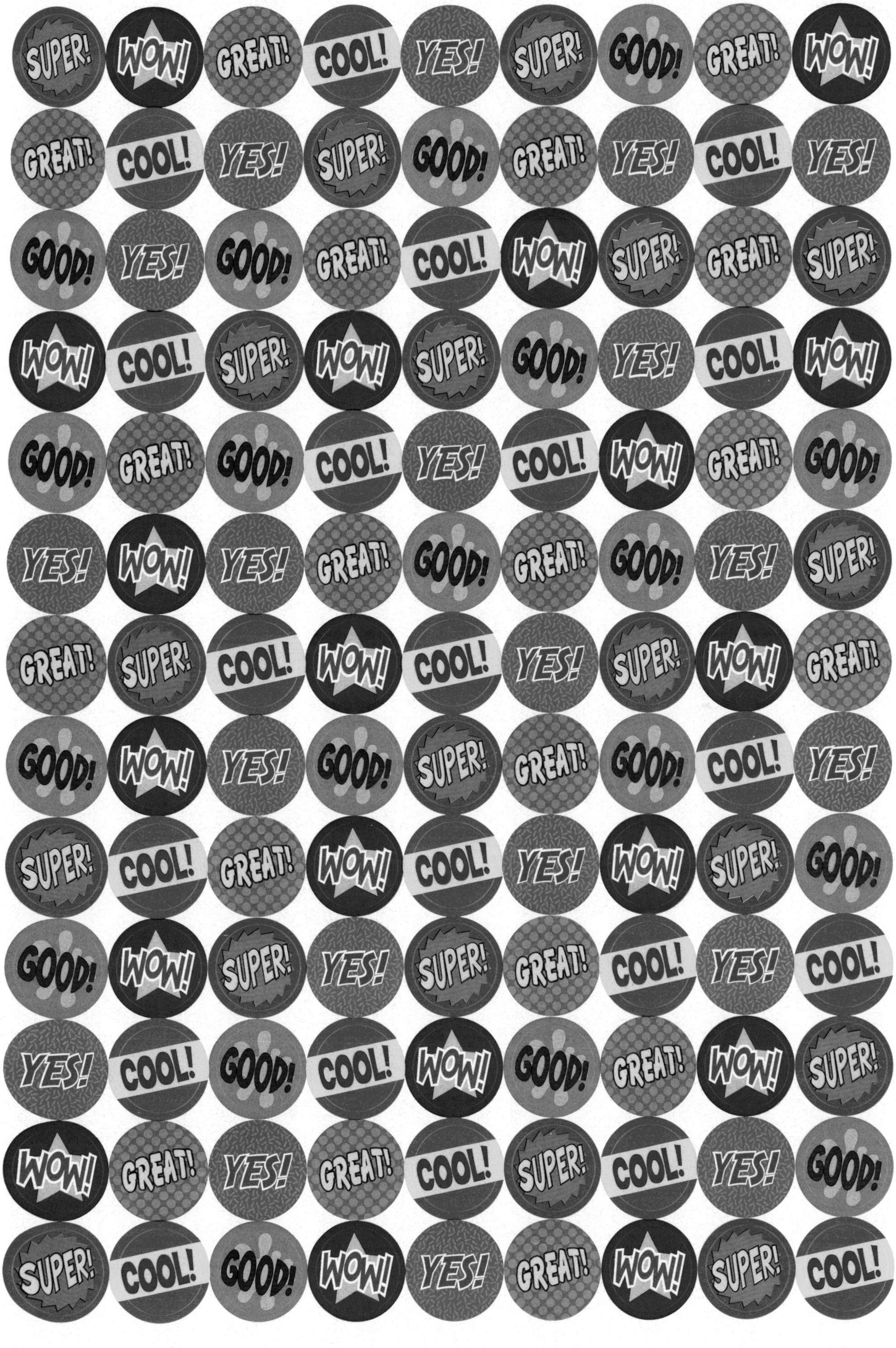

Printed in the U.S.A. PO# 603867 625410